DATE DUE	
JAN 1 9 2005	
MAR 1 7 2005	
AUG 1 5 2006	
AUG 2 9 2006	
SEP 2 6 2006	
MAY 2 4 2007	
GAYLORD	PRINTED IN U.S.A.

Best of Country Potluck
RECIPES

Looking for a New "Dish to Pass"? You're in Luck...Potluck, That is!

GOOD FOOD and good friends are at the heart of any get-together, be it a church hall supper, holiday celebration or other special occasion. With so many events to attend throughout the year, though, coming up with new crowd-pleasing dishes that appeal to a variety of palates can be a challenge.

When you're faced with the "What should I bring this time?" predicament, flip through the pages of this *Best of Country Potluck Recipes* book. It's filled with 244 plate-filling ideas from past issues of *Taste of Home* and its "sister" publications.

Great cooks from across the country shared these sizeable recipes, which have proven most popular for them at all sorts of gatherings. Our test kitchen staff prepared and taste-tested each dish as well, selecting it for a book we call "The Best".

Folks will eagerly wait in line for any of the mouth-watering main dishes featured in this recipe collection, like delicious Stuffed Pasta Shells, pictured on the front cover. Soups and sandwiches are convenient to feed a crowd, so there's some of those to choose from as well.

Signed up to bring a garden-fresh salad or side dish? We've put together a satisfying selection—along with appetizing snacks and beverages and from-scratch breads, rolls and muffins—all great for a group.

If you're looking for recipes with even larger yields, search no further. In the Feeding 50 or More chapter, there's a surefire assortment of dishes you can rely on to feed 50, 150 or any number in between.

And get ready for compliments when you set out any of the delectable desserts found in this cookbook. Not only do they make a pretty presentation on a potluck table—they also will be one of the first to get eaten.

Cooking for a crowd doesn't mean having to sacrifice quality...not when you have *Best of Country Potluck Recipes* in your hands. Make any of the 244 recipes featured in this cookbook next time you need a dish to pass, and watch it disappear fast!

Best of Country Potluck RECIPES

Editor: Jean Steiner
Art Director: Niki Malmberg
Food Editor: Janaan Cunningham
Associate Food Editors: Coleen Martin, Diane Werner
Senior Recipe Editor: Sue A. Jurack
Associate Editor: Julie Schnittka
Food Photography: Rob Hagen, Dan Roberts
Senior Food Photography Artist: Stephanie Marchese
Food Photography Artist: Julie Ferron
Photo Studio Manager: Anne Schimmel
Graphic Art Associates: Ellen Lloyd, Catherine Fletcher
Chairman and Founder: Roy Reiman
President: Tom Curl

©2002 Reiman Media Group, Inc.
5400 S. 60th St., Greendale WI 53129
International Standard Book Number: 0-89821-354-1
Library of Congress Control Number: 2002094599
All rights reserved.
Printed in U.S.A.

Snacks & Beverages

Taco Tater Skins (p. 9)

Chapter 1

Four-Cheese Pate

(Pictured at right)

Jeanne Messina, Darien, Connecticut

This impressive and festive-looking cheese spread is simple to put together and never fails to get raves at parties. Before I retired, I looked for recipes like this that can be prepared way ahead of time.

    3 packages (8 ounces *each*) cream cheese, softened, *divided*
    2 tablespoons milk
    2 tablespoons sour cream
  3/4 cup chopped pecans
    4 ounces Brie *or* Camembert, rind removed, softened
    1 cup (4 ounces) shredded Swiss cheese
    4 ounces crumbled blue cheese
  1/2 cup pecan halves
Red and green apple slices *or* crackers

In a mixing bowl, beat one package of cream cheese with milk and sour cream until smooth. Spread into a 9-in. pie plate lined with plastic wrap. Sprinkle with chopped pecans.

In a mixing bowl, beat Brie, Swiss, blue cheese and remaining cream cheese until thoroughly combined. Gently spread over chopped pecans, smoothing the top to form a flat surface. Cover and chill overnight or up to 3-4 days.

Before serving, invert onto a plate and remove plastic wrap. Arrange pecan halves on top. Serve with apples or crackers. **Yield:** 16-20 servings.

Apricot Wraps

(Pictured below)

Jane Ashworth, Beavercreek, Ohio

I accumulated a large recipe collection from around the world while my husband served in the Air Force for 25 years. This mouth-watering appetizer is one of our favorites, and we enjoy sharing it with friends.

    1 package (14 ounces) dried apricots
  1/2 cup whole almonds
    1 pound sliced bacon
  1/4 cup plum *or* apple jelly
    2 tablespoons soy sauce

Fold each apricot around an almond. Cut bacon strips into thirds; wrap a strip around each apricot and secure with a toothpick. Place on two ungreased 15-in. x 10-in. x 1-in. baking pans. Bake, uncovered, at 375° for 25 minutes or until bacon is crisp, turning once.

In a small saucepan, combine jelly and soy sauce; cook and stir over low heat for 5 minutes or until warmed and smooth. Remove apricots to paper towels; drain. Serve with sauce for dipping. **Yield:** about 4-1/2 dozen.

Easy Black Bean Salsa

Bettie Lake, Scottsdale, Arizona

This salsa is a staple at my house. I can make it in about 5 minutes, so it's great for quick meals or snacks.

    1 can (14-1/2 ounces) Mexican stewed tomatoes
    1 can (15 ounces) black beans, rinsed and drained
    1 can (4 ounces) chopped green chilies, undrained
  1/2 cup chopped onion
  1/4 cup minced fresh cilantro *or* parsley
  1/2 teaspoon salt
    1 can (2-1/4 ounces) sliced ripe olives, drained

Drain tomatoes, reserving juice. Cut up tomatoes; place in a bowl. Add juice and all remaining ingredients; stir until combined. Cover and store in the refrigerator. Serve with tortilla chips or as an accompaniment to Mexican food. **Yield:** about 4 cups.

Crunchy Vegetable Dip

Dottie Miller, Jonesborough, Tennessee

I love to try new recipes, and this one was a big hit with my family. It's great as an appetizer or for a light lunch.

    1 package (8 ounces) cream cheese, softened
    1 tablespoon mayonnaise
    1 tablespoon lemon juice
    1/2 teaspoon salt
    1/8 teaspoon pepper
    3/4 cup grated carrots
    1/2 cup diced celery
    1/2 cup diced cucumber
    1/2 cup diced green pepper
    1/3 cup diced green onions
    Crackers *or* bread

In a mixing bowl, beat cream cheese, mayonnaise, lemon juice, salt and pepper until smooth. Stir in vegetables. Cover; chill for 2-3 hours. Serve with crackers or use as a sandwich spread. **Yield:** about 2 cups.

Mini Hamburgers

Judy Lewis, Sterling Heights, Michigan

I guarantee these will be the first snack cleared from any buffet table. They're that good.

    1/2 cup chopped onion
    1 tablespoon butter *or* margarine
    1 pound lean ground beef
    1 egg, beaten
    1/4 teaspoon seasoned salt
    1/4 teaspoon rubbed sage
    1/4 teaspoon salt
    1/8 teaspoon pepper
    40 mini rolls, split
    8 ounces process American cheese slices, cut
        into 1-1/2-inch squares, optional
    40 dill pickle slices, optional

In a skillet, saute onion in butter. Transfer to a bowl. Add beef, egg and seasonings; mix well. Spread over bottom halves of the rolls; replace tops. Place on baking sheets; cover with foil. Bake at 350° for 20-25 minutes or until meat is no longer pink. If desired, place a cheese square and pickle on each; replace tops and foil. Return to the oven for 5 minutes. **Yield:** 40 appetizers.

Popcorn Nut Crunch

Midge Stolte, Blackfalds, Alberta

Our brood says it's not Christmas here until I make this. I usually double the recipe so I can put some in tins or baskets for hostess gifts when we're invited out.

    2 quarts popped popcorn
    1 cup blanched whole almonds, toasted
    1 cup *each* pecan halves, cashews, Brazil nuts
        and hazelnuts, toasted
    1-1/2 cups sugar

    1 cup dark corn syrup
    1/2 cup butter *or* margarine
    1 teaspoon vanilla extract
    1/2 teaspoon ground cinnamon

Place the popcorn and nuts in a lightly greased 5-qt. Dutch oven. Bake at 250° for 20 minutes. Meanwhile, in a medium saucepan, combine sugar, corn syrup and butter; bring to a boil over medium heat, stirring constantly. Cook, without stirring, until a candy thermometer reads 290° (soft-crack stage).

Remove from the heat; stir in vanilla and cinnamon. Pour a small amount at a time over popcorn mixture, stirring constantly until well coated. Immediately spread on greased baking sheets. Cool; break into pieces. Store in airtight containers. **Yield:** about 4 quarts.

Cold Vegetable Pizza

(Pictured above)

Marlene Reichart, Leesport, Pennsylvania

This is one of my favorite vegetable recipes. I've made it as an hors d'oeuvre for many parties.

    2 tubes (8 ounces *each*) refrigerated crescent rolls
    1 cup mayonnaise
    1 package (8 ounces) cream cheese, softened
    1 tablespoon dill weed
    2-1/2 cups mixed chopped fresh vegetables
        (cucumber, radishes, broccoli, onion, green
        pepper, carrots, celery, mushrooms)
    1/2 cup sliced ripe olives
    3/4 cup shredded cheddar cheese
    3/4 cup shredded mozzarella cheese

Unroll the crescent rolls and place in an ungreased 15-in. x 10-in. x 1-in. baking pan. Flatten dough to fit the pan, sealing seams and perforations. Bake at 375° for 10 minutes or until golden brown. Cool.

In a small mixing bowl, beat the mayonnaise, cream cheese and dill until smooth; spread over crust. Top with the vegetables of your choice. Sprinkle with olives and cheeses; press lightly. Cover and chill for at least 1 hour. Cut into squares. **Yield:** 12-15 servings.

Rye Party Puffs

(Pictured above)

Kelly Thornberry, La Porte, Indiana

I can't go anywhere without taking along my puffs. They're pretty enough for a wedding reception yet also hearty enough to snack on while watching football.

    1 cup water
    1/2 cup butter *or* margarine
    1/2 cup all-purpose flour
    1/2 cup rye flour
    2 teaspoons dried parsley flakes
    1/2 teaspoon garlic powder
    1/4 teaspoon salt
    4 eggs
Caraway seeds
CORNED BEEF FILLING:
    2 packages (8 ounces *each*) cream cheese,
        softened
    2 packages (2-1/2 ounces *each*) thinly sliced
        cooked corned beef, chopped
    1/2 cup mayonnaise
    1/4 cup sour cream
    2 tablespoons minced chives
    2 tablespoons diced onion
    1 teaspoon spicy brown *or* horseradish mustard
    1/8 teaspoon garlic powder
    10 small stuffed olives, chopped

In a saucepan over medium heat, bring water and butter to a boil. Add flours, parsley, garlic powder and salt all at once; stir until a smooth ball forms. Remove from the heat; let stand for 5 minutes. Beat in eggs, one at a time, beating until smooth. Drop batter by rounded teaspoonfuls 2 in. apart onto greased baking sheets. Sprinkle with caraway.

Bake at 400° for 18-20 minutes or until golden. Remove to wire racks. Immediately cut a slit in each puff to allow steam to escape; cool. In a mixing bowl, combine the cream cheese, corned beef, mayonnaise, sour cream, chives, onion, mustard and garlic powder; mix well. Stir in olives. Split puffs; add filling. Refrigerate until serving. **Yield:** 4-1/2 dozen.

Savory Bread Strips

(Pictured at left)

Mary Nichols, Dover, New Hampshire

The savory ingredients in this irresistible appetizer blend so well that I'm always asked for the recipe.

- 1 package (1/4 ounce) active dry yeast
- 6-1/2 teaspoons sugar, *divided*
- 1/2 cup warm water (110° to 115°)
- 3 tablespoons olive *or* vegetable oil
- 2 tablespoons dried minced onion
- 2 teaspoons dried basil
- 1 teaspoon dried oregano
- 1 teaspoon rubbed sage
- 1 teaspoon garlic powder
- 1/2 cup cold water
- 3 cups all-purpose flour

TOPPING:
- 1-1/2 cups chopped fully cooked ham
- 1 cup shredded Parmesan cheese
- 1/2 cup chopped ripe olives
- 1/2 cup chopped onion
- 1/2 cup minced fresh parsley
- 1/4 cup olive *or* vegetable oil
- 2 garlic cloves, minced

Dissolve yeast and 1/2 teaspoon sugar in warm water; set aside. In a saucepan, combine oil, onion, basil, oregano, sage and garlic powder; cook over medium heat for 1 minute. Remove from the heat; stir in cold water. In a mixing bowl, combine flour and remaining sugar. Stir in oil and yeast mixtures.

Turn onto a lightly floured surface; knead for 3 minutes. Place dough on a greased 15-in. x 10-in. x 1-in. baking pan. Cover and let stand for 15 minutes. Pat dough evenly into pan. Combine topping ingredients; sprinkle over dough. Bake at 375° for 25-30 minutes or until well browned. Cut into 2-in. x 1-in. strips. **Yield:** about 6 dozen.

Taco Tater Skins

Phyllis Douglas, Fairview, Michigan

We make a meal out of these skins. But they're also great for parties as appetizers.

- 6 large russet potatoes
- 1/2 cup butter *or* margarine, melted
- 2 tablespoons taco seasoning
- 1 cup (4 ounces) shredded cheddar cheese
- 15 bacon strips, cooked and crumbled
- 3 green onions, chopped

Salsa *and/or* sour cream

Bake potatoes at 375° for 1 hour or until tender. Reduce heat to 350°. When cool enough to handle, cut the potatoes lengthwise into quarters. Scoop out pulp, leaving a 1/4-in. shell (save pulp for another use).

Combine the butter and taco seasoning; brush over both sides of potato skins. Place skin side down on a greased baking sheet. Sprinkle with cheese, bacon and onions. Bake for 5-10 minutes or until the cheese is melted. Serve with salsa and/or sour cream. **Yield:** 2 dozen.

Spiced Nut Mix

Patti Holland, Parker, Colorado

A good friend gave me a special gift one Christmas— this recipe and a sack of ingredients. I think of her every time I stir up this mix.

- 3 egg whites
- 2 teaspoons water
- 2 cans (12 ounces *each*) salted peanuts
- 1 cup whole blanched almonds
- 1 cup walnut halves
- 1-3/4 cups sugar
- 3 tablespoons pumpkin pie spice
- 3/4 teaspoon salt
- 1 cup raisins

In a mixing bowl, beat egg whites and water until frothy. Add nuts; stir gently to coat. Combine sugar, pie spice and salt; add to nut mixture and stir gently to coat. Fold in raisins. Spread into two greased 15-in. x 10-in. x 1-in. baking pans. Bake, uncovered, at 300° for 20-25 minutes or until lightly browned, stirring every 10 minutes. Cool. Store in an airtight container. **Yield:** about 10 cups.

Bacon-Broccoli Cheese Ball

(Pictured below)

Tamara Rickard, Bartlett, Tennessee

Needing an appetizer one night when dinner was running late, I came up with this cheese ball. For variety, substitute favorite herbs for the pepper.

- 1 package (8 ounces) cream cheese, softened
- 1 cup (4 ounces) shredded cheddar cheese
- 1/2 teaspoon pepper
- 1 cup finely chopped broccoli florets
- 6 bacon strips, cooked and crumbled

Assorted crackers

In a mixing bowl, beat cream cheese, cheddar cheese and pepper until blended. Stir in broccoli. Shape into a ball and roll in bacon. Cover and refrigerate. Remove from the refrigerator 15 minutes before serving. Serve with crackers. **Yield:** 2-1/2 cups.

Christmas Party Pinwheels

Janis Plourde, Smooth Rock Falls, Ontario

These pinwheels look so special and pretty that folks can't resist them! The refreshing flavor of ranch dressing and crisp colorful vegetables makes them a pleasure to serve.

- 2 packages (8 ounces *each*) cream cheese, softened
- 1 package (.4 ounce) ranch salad dressing mix
- 1/2 cup minced sweet red pepper
- 1/2 cup minced celery
- 1/4 cup sliced green onions
- 1/4 cup sliced stuffed olives
- 3 to 4 flour tortillas (10 inches)

In a mixing bowl, beat cream cheese and dressing mix until smooth. Add red pepper, celery, onions and olives; mix well. Spread about 3/4 cup on each tortilla. Roll up tightly; wrap in plastic wrap. Refrigerate for at least 2 hours. Slice into 1/2-in. pieces. **Yield:** 15-20 servings.

Hot Pizza Dip

(Pictured below)

Karen Riordan, Fern Creek, Kentucky

I love this recipe because it's easy to prepare in advance and keep refrigerated. Put it in the oven when guests arrive, and by the time you've poured beverages, the dip is ready. It gets gobbled up quickly!

- 1 package (8 ounces) cream cheese, softened
- 1 teaspoon Italian seasoning
- 1/4 teaspoon garlic powder
- 2 cups (8 ounces) shredded mozzarella cheese
- 1 cup (4 ounces) shredded cheddar cheese
- 1/2 cup pizza sauce

- 1/2 cup finely chopped green pepper
- 1/2 cup finely chopped sweet red pepper
- Tortilla chips *or* breadsticks

In a bowl, combine cream cheese, Italian seasoning and garlic powder; spread on the bottom of a greased 9-in. pie plate. Combine cheeses; sprinkle half over the cream cheese layer. Top with the pizza sauce and peppers. Sprinkle with the remaining cheeses. Bake at 350° for 20 minutes. Serve warm with tortilla chips or breadsticks. **Yield:** about 3-1/2 cups.

Favorite Snack Mix

Carol Allen, McLeansboro, Illinois

For a great change of pace from the usual mix, try this recipe. It's almost impossible to stop eating this sweet and salty snack.

- 6 cups Crispix cereal
- 1 can (10 ounces) mixed nuts
- 1 package (10 ounces) pretzel sticks
- 3/4 cup butter *or* margarine
- 3/4 cup packed brown sugar

In a large bowl, combine the cereal, nuts and pretzels. In a small saucepan over low heat, melt butter. Add brown sugar; cook and stir until dissolved. Pour over cereal mixture; stir to coat.

Place a third on a greased 15-in. x 10-in. x 1-in. baking pan. Bake at 325° for 8 minutes; stir and bake for 6 minutes more. Spread on waxed paper to cool. Repeat with remaining mixture. Store in an airtight container. **Yield:** about 14 cups.

Appetizer Meatballs

Pat Waymire, Yellow Springs, Ohio

These tasty meatballs are a perennial favorite at our Christmas parties.

- 1 egg, lightly beaten
- 1/2 cup soft bread crumbs
- 1/4 cup milk
- 1/3 cup finely chopped onion
- 1 teaspoon salt
- 1/2 teaspoon Worcestershire sauce
- 1 pound ground beef

SAUCE:
- 1/2 cup ketchup
- 1/2 cup chopped onion
- 1/3 cup sugar
- 1/3 cup vinegar
- 1 tablespoon Worcestershire sauce
- 1/8 teaspoon pepper

Combine the first six ingredients; crumble beef over mixture and mix well. Shape into 1-in. balls. In a skillet over medium heat, brown meatballs; drain. Place in a 2-1/2-qt. baking dish. Combine sauce ingredients. Pour over meatballs. Bake, uncovered, at 350° for 50-60 minutes or until meatballs are no longer pink. **Yield:** about 3 dozen.

Sausage Quiche Squares

Linda Wheeler, Middleburg, Florida

Having done some catering, I especially appreciate interesting, appetizing finger foods. I'm constantly asked to make these popular squares to serve at parties.

- 1 pound bulk pork sausage
- 1 cup (4 ounces) shredded cheddar cheese
- 1 cup (4 ounces) shredded Monterey Jack cheese
- 1/2 cup finely chopped onion
- 1 can (4 ounces) chopped green chilies
- 1 tablespoon minced jalapeno pepper,* optional
- 10 eggs
- 1 teaspoon chili powder
- 1 teaspoon ground cumin
- 1 teaspoon salt
- 1/2 teaspoon garlic powder
- 1/2 teaspoon pepper

In a large skillet, cook sausage until no longer pink; drain. Place in a greased 13-in. x 9-in. x 2-in. baking dish. Layer with cheeses, onion, chilies and jalapeno if desired. In a bowl, beat eggs and seasonings. Pour over cheese. Bake, uncovered, at 375° for 18-22 minutes or until a knife inserted near the center comes out clean. Cool for 10 minutes; cut into 1-in. squares. **Yield:** about 8 dozen.

*Editor's Note: When cutting or seeding hot peppers, use rubber or plastic gloves to protect your hands. Avoid touching your face.

- 1 cup mayonnaise
- 2 teaspoons dried minced onion
- 2 teaspoons ground mustard
- 1 cup crushed butter-flavored crackers
- 1/2 cup sesame seeds
- 2 pounds boneless skinless chicken breasts

SAUCE:
- 1 cup mayonnaise
- 2 tablespoons honey

In a bowl, combine mayonnaise, onion and mustard. In another bowl, combine the crackers and sesame seeds. Cut chicken lengthwise into 1/4-in. strips. Dip strips into mayonnaise mixture, then into the sesame seed mixture. Place in a single layer on a large greased baking sheet. Bake at 425° for 15-18 minutes or until juices run clear. Combine sauce ingredients and serve with chicken strips. **Yield:** 10-12 servings.

Sesame Chicken Strips

(Pictured below)

Teri Rasey, Cadillac, Michigan

These tasty chicken strips dipped in the lightly sweet sauce are a wonderful finger food. They go over really well at outdoor summer gatherings. This recipe puts a new twist on fried chicken—a staple at most picnics.

Toasted Zucchini Snacks

(Pictured above)

Jane Bone, Cape Coral, Florida

I added green pepper to this recipe I got years ago from a friend. I prepare this rich snack for company when zucchini is plentiful. Everyone seems to enjoy it—even those who say they don't care for zucchini.

- 2 cups shredded zucchini
- 1 teaspoon salt
- 1/2 cup mayonnaise *or* salad dressing
- 1/2 cup plain yogurt
- 1/4 cup grated Parmesan cheese
- 1/4 cup finely chopped green pepper
- 4 green onions, thinly sliced
- 1 garlic clove, minced
- 1 teaspoon Worcestershire sauce
- 1/4 teaspoon hot pepper sauce
- 36 slices snack rye bread

In a bowl, toss the zucchini and salt; let stand for 1 hour. Rinse and drain, pressing out excess liquid. Add the next eight ingredients; stir until combined. Spread a rounded teaspoonful on each slice of bread; place on a baking sheet. Bake at 375° for 10-12 minutes or until bubbly. **Yield:** 3 dozen.

Holiday Wassail

Lucy Meyring, Walden, Colorado

I serve this drink every year for Christmas. Warm and fruity, this richly colored beverage is easy to make and is a festive addition to dinner.

    1 quart hot tea
    1 cup sugar
    1 bottle (32 ounces) cranberry juice
    1 bottle (32 ounces) apple juice
    2 cups orange juice
  3/4 cup lemon juice
    2 cinnamon sticks (3 inches *each*)
   24 whole cloves, *divided*
    1 orange, sliced

In a large kettle, combine tea and sugar. Add juices, cinnamon sticks and 12 of the cloves. Bring to a boil and boil for 2 minutes. Remove from the heat. Serve warm or cool. Garnish punch bowl with orange slices studded with remaining cloves. **Yield:** 12-16 servings (1 gallon).

Aunt Frances' Lemonade

(Pictured above)

Debbie Blackburn, Camp Hill, Pennsylvania

My sister and I spent a week each summer with Aunt Frances, who always had this thirst-quenching lemonade in a stoneware crock in the refrigerator. It tastes so much like fresh citrus. It made such a refreshing drink after a hot day running around the farm.

    5 lemons
    5 limes
    5 oranges
    3 quarts water
  1-1/2 to 2 cups sugar

Squeeze juice from four of the lemons, limes and oranges; pour into a gallon container. Thinly slice remaining fruit and set aside for garnish. Add water and sugar to juices; mix well. Store in refrigerator. Serve on ice with fruit slices. **Yield:** 12-16 servings (about 1 gallon).

Beverage Basics

ONE of the easiest ways to keep a large punch bowl cold is to make large ice cubes in coated paper milk cartons (remove the paper label before using). The larger the ice cube, the slower it will melt.

Pretty glass mugs make a great presentation for hot drinks. To prevent the glass from cracking, simply place a dinner spoon in the mug and slowly pour the hot liquid onto the spoon.

Mocha Punch

(Pictured below)

Yvonne Hatfield, Norman, Oklahoma

I first tried this smooth creamy punch at a friend's Christmas open house a number of years ago. It was so special and distinctive, I didn't leave the party until I had a copy of the recipe. Having a frosty glass of this choco-

late punch is almost like sipping a chocolate shake. It's a nice change from traditional fruit punches.

1-1/2 quarts water
1/2 cup instant chocolate drink mix
1/2 cup sugar
1/4 cup instant coffee granules
1/2 gallon vanilla ice cream
1/2 gallon chocolate ice cream
1 cup whipping cream, whipped
Chocolate curls, optional

In a large saucepan, bring water to a boil. Remove from the heat. Add drink mix, sugar and coffee; stir until dissolved. Cover and refrigerate for 4 hours or overnight.

About 30 minutes before serving, pour into a punch bowl. Add ice cream by scoopfuls; stir until partially melted. Garnish with dollops of whipped cream and chocolate curls if desired. **Yield:** 20-25 servings.

Cherry Punch

Davlyn Jones, San Jose, California

Back in 1952, a co-worker gave me the recipe for this versatile rosy punch. It's not too sweet, so it really refreshes. My family and friends have sipped it at countless gatherings, from picnics to the holidays, over the years.

1 can (6 ounces) frozen lemonade concentrate, thawed
1 can (6 ounces) frozen limeade concentrate, thawed
1 can (20 ounces) pineapple chunks, undrained
2 cups water
2 liters cherry soda, chilled
2 liters ginger ale, chilled
Lemon and lime slices, optional

In a blender, combine concentrates and pineapple; cover and blend until smooth. Pour into a gallon-size container; stir in water. Store in the refrigerator. To serve, pour the mixture into a punch bowl; add cherry soda and ginger ale. Garnish with lemon and lime slices if desired. **Yield:** about 6 quarts.

Springtime Punch

Janet Mooberry, Peoria, Illinois

Its blend of lemon, orange and pineapple juices defines the sunny color and fruity flavor, while ginger ale adds zesty fizz to this beverage.

2 cups sugar
2-1/2 cups water
1 cup fresh lemon juice (3 to 4 lemons)
1 cup fresh orange juice (2 to 3 oranges)
1 can (6 ounces) frozen pineapple juice concentrate, thawed
2 quarts ginger ale, chilled

In a saucepan, bring sugar and water to a boil. Boil for 10 minutes; remove from the heat. Stir in the lemon,

orange and pineapple juices. Refrigerate. Just before serving, combine with ginger ale in a large punch bowl. **Yield:** 16-20 servings (3 quarts).

Rhubarb Slush

(Pictured below)

Theresa Pearson, Ogilvie, Minnesota

This thirst-quenching slush is a fun way to use rhubarb. I love to serve it for special get-togethers like a ladies' brunch or holiday meal. The tangy flavor of this favorite spring crop comes through in every sip.

3 cups chopped fresh *or* frozen rhubarb
1 cup water
1/3 cup sugar
1 cup apple juice
1 can (6 ounces) frozen pink lemonade concentrate, thawed
2 liters lemon-lime soda

In a saucepan, combine rhubarb, water and sugar; bring to a boil. Reduce heat; cover and simmer for 5 minutes or until rhubarb is tender. Cool for about 30 minutes. In a food processor or blender, puree mixture, half at a time. Stir in apple juice and lemonade. Pour into a freezer container; cover and freeze until firm.

Let stand at room temperature for 45 minutes before serving. For individual servings, scoop 1/3 cup mixture into a glass and fill with soda. To serve a group, place all of mixture in a large pitcher or punch bowl; add soda and stir. Serve immediately. **Yield:** about 10 servings.

Salads

Asparagus Tomato Salad (p. 21)

Chapter 2

Minted Melon Salad

(Pictured above)

Terry Saylor, Vermillion, South Dakota

People can't resist digging into a salad made with colorful summer fruits. The unique dressing is what makes this salad a crowd-pleaser. I get compliments whenever I serve it, especially when I put it on the table in a melon boat. It's a warm-weather treat.

    1 cup water
  3/4 cup sugar
    3 tablespoons lime juice
1-1/2 teaspoons chopped fresh mint
  3/4 teaspoon aniseed
Pinch salt
    5 cups cubed watermelon (about 1/2 medium melon)
    3 cups cubed cantaloupe (about 1 medium melon)
    3 cups cubed honeydew (about 1 medium melon)
    2 cups peach slices (about 2 peaches)
    1 cup fresh blueberries

In a small saucepan, bring the first six ingredients to a boil. Boil for 2 minutes; remove from the heat. Cover and cool syrup completely. Combine the fruit in a large bowl; add syrup and stir to coat. Cover and chill for at least 2 hours, stirring occasionally. Drain before serving. **Yield:** 12-14 servings.

Layered Chicken Salad

Kay Bridgeman, Lexington, Ohio

This cool main-dish salad really hits the spot during the summer months. Plus, its colorful layers look so appealing. Served with a roll, it's a complete meal.

    3 cups cubed cooked chicken, *divided*
    2 cups torn lettuce

    1 cup cooked long grain rice
    1 package (10 ounces) frozen peas, thawed
  1/4 cup minced fresh parsley
    2 large tomatoes, seeded and chopped
    1 cup thinly sliced cucumber
    1 small sweet red pepper, chopped
    1 small green pepper, chopped
DRESSING:
    1 cup mayonnaise
  1/2 cup sour cream
  1/2 cup raisins
  1/2 cup finely chopped onion
  1/4 cup sweet pickle relish
    2 tablespoons milk
  1/2 teaspoon celery seed
  1/2 teaspoon dill seed
  1/2 teaspoon ground mustard
  1/2 teaspoon garlic salt
Sweet red pepper rings and fresh parsley sprigs, optional

In a 3-qt. glass bowl, layer 1-1/2 cups chicken and the lettuce. Combine the rice, peas and parsley; spoon over lettuce. Layer with tomatoes, cucumber, peppers and remaining chicken.

Combine the first 10 dressing ingredients; spoon over salad. Garnish with red pepper rings and fresh parsley if desired. Cover and refrigerate for 8 hours or overnight. **Yield:** 10-12 servings.

Vegetable Cheese Salad

Shary Geidner, Clear Lake, Iowa

Here's a satisfying salad that's garden-fresh. It stars three delicious cheeses and refreshing vegetables like crisp cucumber, bell peppers and juicy tomatoes. This unique salad makes a nice light lunch or super side dish anytime of year.

    3 cups (12 ounces) shredded cheddar, Monterey Jack *and/or* mozzarella cheese
    1 medium cucumber, chopped
    1 medium tomato, seeded and chopped
    1 green onion, thinly sliced
  1/2 cup chopped green pepper
  1/2 cup chopped sweet red pepper
  1/2 cup sour cream
  1/4 cup mayonnaise
    1 tablespoon lemon juice
    1 tablespoon lime juice
    1 garlic clove, minced
  1/2 teaspoon Dijon mustard
  1/2 teaspoon dried basil
  1/2 teaspoon dried marjoram
  1/2 teaspoon paprika
  1/2 teaspoon sugar
Lettuce, optional

In a bowl, combine cheeses, cucumber, tomato, onion and peppers. In a small bowl, combine sour cream, mayonnaise, lemon and lime juice, garlic, mustard and seasonings; mix well. Pour over salad and toss to coat. Chill for 1 hour. Serve in a lettuce-lined bowl if desired. **Yield:** 16 servings.

Parmesan Vegetable Toss

Judy Barbato, N. Easton, Massachusetts

The first time I made this salad it was with two others for a Fourth of July party years ago. This one disappeared long before the other two!

        2 cups mayonnaise *or* salad dressing
    1/2 cup grated Parmesan cheese
    1/4 cup sugar
    1/2 teaspoon dried basil
    1/2 teaspoon salt
        4 cups fresh broccoli florets (about 3/4 pound)
        4 cups fresh cauliflowerets (about 3/4 pound)
        1 medium red onion, sliced
        1 can (8 ounces) sliced water chestnuts, drained
        1 large head iceberg lettuce, torn
        1 pound sliced bacon, cooked and crumbled
        2 cups croutons

In a bowl, combine mayonnaise, Parmesan cheese, sugar, basil and salt. Add broccoli, cauliflower, onion and water chestnuts; toss. Cover and refrigerate for several hours or overnight. Just before serving, place lettuce in a salad bowl and top with vegetable mixture. Sprinkle with bacon. Top with croutons. **Yield:** 16-18 servings.

Layered Basil Salad

(Pictured below)

Marcy Cella, L'Anse, Michigan

The colorful ingredients in this salad look beautiful and taste wonderful together. It's especially impressive on a potluck buffet.

        4 cups torn assorted salad greens
        4 medium carrots, julienned
    1-1/2 cups cooked macaroni shells
        2 cups frozen peas, thawed
        1 medium red onion, diced
    3/4 pound fully cooked ham, cubed
    1/3 cup shredded Swiss cheese
    1/3 cup shredded cheddar cheese
DRESSING:
        1 cup mayonnaise
    1/2 cup sour cream

        2 teaspoons Dijon mustard
    1-1/2 teaspoons chopped fresh basil *or* 1/2 teaspoon
            dried basil
    1/2 teaspoon salt
    1/4 teaspoon pepper
        2 hard-cooked eggs, cut into wedges, optional

In a 3-1/2-qt. glass bowl, layer greens, carrots, macaroni, peas, onion, ham and cheeses. In a small bowl, combine the first six dressing ingredients; spread over salad. Garnish with eggs if desired. Cover and chill for several hours. **Yield:** 12-14 servings.

Antipasto Salad

(Pictured above)

Agnes Bulkley, Hicksville, New York

I take this fresh-tasting, colorful salad to potluck dinners throughout the year, since everyone who tries it loves it. It's a nice hearty dish.

        1 package (16 ounces) rotini pasta
        1 can (15 ounces) garbanzo beans, rinsed and
            drained
        1 package (3-1/2 ounces) sliced pepperoni,
            halved
        1 can (2-1/4 ounces) sliced ripe olives, drained
    1/2 cup diced sweet red pepper
    1/2 cup diced green pepper
        4 medium fresh mushrooms, sliced
        2 garlic cloves, minced
        2 tablespoons minced fresh basil *or* 2 teaspoons
            dried basil
        2 teaspoons salt
    1-1/2 teaspoons minced fresh oregano *or* 1/2
            teaspoon dried oregano
    1/2 teaspoon pepper
    1/4 teaspoon cayenne pepper
        1 cup olive *or* vegetable oil
    2/3 cup lemon juice

Cook the pasta according to package directions; drain and rinse with cold water. Place in a large salad bowl. Add the next 12 ingredients; mix well. In a jar with tight-fitting lid, shake oil and lemon juice. Pour over salad and toss. Cover and refrigerate 6 hours or overnight. Stir before serving. **Yield:** 12-16 servings.

Summer Spaghetti Salad

Lucia Johnson, Massena, New York

This attractive, fresh-tasting salad can conveniently be made the night before. The recipe yields a big bowl!

☑ Uses less fat, sugar or salt. Includes Nutritional Analysis and Diabetic Exchanges.

- 1 package (16 ounces) thin spaghetti, broken in half
- 3 medium tomatoes, diced
- 3 small zucchini, diced
- 1 large cucumber, halved, seeded and diced
- 1 medium green pepper, diced
- 1 medium sweet red pepper, diced
- 1 bottle (8 ounces) Italian salad dressing
- 2 tablespoons grated Parmesan cheese
- 1-1/2 teaspoons sesame seeds
- 1-1/2 teaspoons poppy seeds
- 1/2 teaspoon paprika
- 1/4 teaspoon celery seed
- 1/8 teaspoon garlic powder

Cook spaghetti according to package directions; drain and rinse in cold water. Place in a large bowl; add tomatoes, zucchini, cucumber and peppers. Combine remaining ingredients; pour over salad. Toss to coat. Cover and refrigerate for 2 hours. **Yield:** 16 servings.

Nutritional Analysis: One 1-cup serving (prepared with fat-free salad dressing and reduced-fat Parmesan cheese topping) equals 137 calories, 150 mg sodium, trace cholesterol, 27 gm carbohydrate, 5 gm protein, 1 gm fat. **Diabetic Exchanges:** 1-1/2 starch, 1 vegetable.

Two-Cheese Tossed Salad

(Pictured below)

Barbara Birk, American Fork, Utah

Colorful, hearty ingredients and a delectable dressing make second helpings of this salad hard to resist.

- 1/2 cup vegetable oil
- 1/2 cup chopped red onion
- 1/4 cup sugar

- 1/4 cup vinegar
- 1 teaspoon poppy seeds
- 1/2 teaspoon dried minced onion
- 1/4 to 1/2 teaspoon prepared mustard
- 1/8 to 1/4 teaspoon salt
- 5 cups torn fresh spinach
- 5 cups torn iceberg lettuce
- 1/2 pound fresh mushrooms, sliced
- 1 carton (8 ounces) cottage cheese
- 1 cup (4 ounces) shredded Swiss cheese
- 2 bacon strips, cooked and crumbled

In a jar with tight-fitting lid, combine the first eight ingredients. Refrigerate overnight. Just before serving, toss spinach, lettuce, mushrooms and cheeses in a large salad bowl. Shake dressing and pour over salad. Sprinkle with bacon. **Yield:** 12-14 servings.

Orange Tapioca Salad

Denise Nebel, Wayland, Iowa

Fresh, fruity flavor makes this pretty salad popular with all ages. Our whole family really digs into its fluffy goodness. I can put it together in the morning or even the night before and pop it in the fridge until suppertime.

- 3 cups water
- 1 package (3 ounces) orange gelatin
- 1 package (3.4 ounces) instant vanilla pudding mix
- 1 package (3 ounces) tapioca pudding mix
- 1 can (15 ounces) mandarin oranges, drained
- 1 can (8 ounces) crushed pineapple, drained
- 1 carton (8 ounces) frozen whipped topping, thawed

In a saucepan, bring water to a boil. Whisk in gelatin and pudding mixes. Return to a boil, stirring constantly; boil for 1 minute. Remove from the heat and cool completely. Fold in oranges, pineapple and whipped topping. Spoon into a serving bowl. Cover and refrigerate for 2 hours. **Yield:** 12-14 servings.

Green Salad with Onion Dressing

Cara Bonnema, Painesville, Ohio

This is such an elegant salad. It will dress up any table. The caramelized onion in the dressing tastes fantastic. It's never failed to be a hit whenever I've served it.

- 1 large onion, peeled and cut into eighths
- 8 tablespoons olive *or* vegetable oil, *divided*
- 1-1/2 teaspoons sugar
- 1/4 cup chicken broth
- 2 tablespoons cider *or* white wine vinegar
- 1/4 teaspoon salt
- 14 cups torn salad greens
- 1 cup chopped walnuts, toasted
- 1/2 cup thinly sliced red onion

Place onion in a baking dish. Drizzle with 1 tablespoon oil; sprinkle with sugar. Bake, uncovered, at 400° for 30 minutes. Turn and bake 25-30 minutes longer, stirring several times, until the onion is tender and lightly browned. Cool for 30 minutes.

Place onion in a blender or food processor; add broth, vinegar, salt and remaining oil. Cover and process until smooth (mixture will be thick). Chill. Just before serving, toss greens, walnuts, red onion and dressing in a large salad bowl. **Yield:** 12 servings.

Overnight Fruit Salad

(Pictured above)

Eileen Duffeck, Lena, Wisconsin

I first tasted this rich salad at my wedding reception almost 40 years ago. The ladies who did the cooking wouldn't share the recipe at the time, but I eventually got it. I've made it for many meals...and our daughters copied the recipe when they married.

- 3 eggs, beaten
- 1/4 cup sugar
- 1/4 cup vinegar
- 2 tablespoons butter *or* margarine
- 2 cups green grapes
- 2 cups miniature marshmallows
- 1 can (20 ounces) pineapple chunks, drained
- 1 can (15 ounces) mandarin oranges, drained
- 2 medium firm bananas, sliced
- 2 cups whipping cream, whipped
- 1/2 cup chopped pecans

In a double boiler over medium heat, cook and stir eggs, sugar and vinegar until mixture is thickened and reaches 160°. Remove from the heat; stir in butter. Cool. In a large serving bowl, combine grapes, marshmallows,

pineapple, oranges and bananas; add cooled dressing and stir to coat. Refrigerate for 4 hours or overnight. Just before serving, fold in whipped cream and pecans. **Yield:** 12-16 servings.

Grilled Three-Pepper Salad

(Pictured below)

Ruth Wickard, York, Pennsylvania

I have been cooking since my mother taught me how at an early age. I enjoy it, and I'm always trying new recipes. This one's both flavorful and colorful.

- 2 *each* large green, sweet red and yellow peppers, cut into 1-inch pieces
- 1 large red onion, halved and thinly sliced
- 1 pound bulk mozzarella cheese, cut into bite-size cubes
- 1 can (6 ounces) pitted ripe olives, drained and halved

VINAIGRETTE:
- 2/3 cup olive *or* vegetable oil
- 1/3 cup cider *or* red wine vinegar
- 2 tablespoons lemon juice
- 2 tablespoons Dijon mustard
- 1 tablespoon minced fresh basil *or* 1 teaspoon dried basil
- 1/2 teaspoon cayenne pepper
- 1/2 teaspoon garlic powder

Thread peppers onto metal or soaked wooden skewers; grill or broil for 10-12 minutes or until edges are browned. Remove from skewers and place in a large bowl. Add onion, mozzarella and olives; toss gently. Cover and refrigerate.

Combine vinaigrette ingredients in a jar with tight-fitting lid; shake well. Pour over the pepper mixture just before serving; toss to coat. **Yield:** 10-12 servings.

Hot German Potato Salad

(Pictured at right)

Inez Senner, Glendive, Montana

Being single, I enjoy sharing favorite dishes at church and family potlucks. This one has won raves whenever I've served it. I've also found it makes a good lunch that's better the second time around!

- 9 medium potatoes
- 1-1/2 pounds smoked sausage *or* precooked bratwurst
- 6 bacon strips
- 3/4 cup chopped onion
- 2 tablespoons all-purpose flour
- 1 teaspoon salt
- 1/2 teaspoon celery seed
- 1/8 teaspoon pepper
- 1/4 cup sugar
- 1-1/3 cups water
- 2/3 cup cider vinegar

In a saucepan, cook potatoes in boiling salted water until tender. Meanwhile, cut sausage into 1/2-in. slices; saute in a skillet until browned. Drain and place in a large bowl. Drain potatoes; peel and cut into 3/4-in. cubes. Add to sausage; keep warm.

Cook bacon until crisp; crumble and set aside. Drain all but 3 tablespoons of drippings; saute onion in drippings until tender. Stir in the flour, salt, celery seed and pepper; blend well. Add sugar, water and vinegar; bring to a boil. Boil for 2 minutes. Pour over potato mixture and stir gently to coat. Sprinkle with bacon. Serve warm. **Yield:** 12-14 servings.

Crunchy Turkey Salad

Brenda Moore James, Livermore, California

The water chestnuts, almonds, celery and chow mein noodles in this refreshing salad provide lots of crunch. Topping it all is a sweet-sour dressing my family loves.

- 1/4 cup sugar
- 1/4 cup vegetable oil
- 1/4 cup cider *or* red wine vinegar
- 1/2 teaspoon salt
- 1/2 teaspoon garlic salt
- 1/2 teaspoon pepper
- 5 cups cubed cooked turkey, chicken *or* ham
- 6 cups shredded lettuce
- 1 can (8 ounces) sliced water chestnuts, drained
- 2 celery ribs, sliced
- 4 green onions, sliced
- 2 tablespoons sesame seeds, toasted
- 2 tablespoons sliced almonds, toasted
- 1 can (3 ounces) chow mein noodles

In a jar with tight-fitting lid, combine the sugar, oil, vinegar, salt, garlic salt and pepper; cover and shake well. In a large bowl, combine all of the remaining ingredients. Just before serving, add the dressing and toss to coat. **Yield:** 16 servings.

That Good Salad

Betty Lamb, Orem, Utah

When a friend shared this recipe with me, it had a fancy French name. Our children can never remember it, so they say, "Mom, please make 'that good salad'." Now our friends and neighbors request it for parties and potluck dinners.

- 3/4 cup vegetable oil
- 1/4 cup fresh lemon juice
- 2 garlic cloves, minced
- 1/2 teaspoon salt
- 1/2 teaspoon pepper
- 2 bunches (1 pound *each*) romaine, torn
- 2 cups chopped tomatoes
- 1 cup (4 ounces) shredded Swiss cheese
- 2/3 cup slivered almonds, toasted, optional
- 1/2 cup grated Parmesan cheese
- 8 bacon strips, cooked and crumbled
- 1 cup Caesar salad croutons

In a jar with tight-fitting lid, combine oil, lemon juice, garlic, salt and pepper; cover and shake well. Chill. In a bowl, toss romaine, tomatoes, Swiss cheese, almonds if desired, Parmesan cheese and bacon. Shake dressing; pour over salad and toss. Add croutons and serve immediately. **Yield:** 14 servings.

Tart Cherry Salad

Bea Wittman, Ridgway, Pennsylvania

This salad recipe has been in my family for a number of years; we especially use it during the holiday season. It's pleasantly tart and a perfect complement to any meal throughout the year.

- 2 cans (16 ounces *each*) tart red cherries
- 2 cans (8 ounces *each*) crushed pineapple
- 1 cup sugar
- 2 packages (6 ounces *each*) cherry gelatin
- 3 cups ginger ale
- 3/4 cup flaked coconut
- 1 cup chopped nuts, optional

Drain cherries and pineapple, reserving juices. Set fruit aside. Add enough water to combined juices to make 3-1/4 cups; pour into a saucepan. Add sugar; bring to a boil. Remove from the heat; stir in gelatin until dissolved. Add cherries, pineapple and ginger ale. Chill until partially set. Stir in coconut and nuts if desired. Pour into a 3-qt. mold or 13-in. x 9-in. x 2-in. pan coated with nonstick cooking spray. Chill until firm, about 3 hours. **Yield:** 16-18 servings.

Wild Rice Salad

(Pictured below)

Lyn Graebert, Park Falls, Wisconsin

Since cranberries grow well in this area, I love to use the dried variety to give recipes like this hearty salad color and tang.

 Uses less fat, sugar or salt. Includes Nutritional Analysis and Diabetic Exchanges.

- 4 cups cooked wild rice
- 1 can (8 ounces) sliced water chestnuts, drained and chopped
- 1/2 cup thinly sliced celery
- 1/2 cup chopped green pepper
- 1/2 cup frozen peas, thawed
- 1/2 cup dried cranberries
- 1/4 cup thinly sliced green onions
- 1/4 cup minced fresh parsley
- 1/3 cup cranberry juice
- 1/3 cup vinegar
- 2 teaspoons olive *or* vegetable oil
- 3/4 teaspoon dried basil
- 3/4 teaspoon sugar
- 3/4 teaspoon salt, optional
- 1/4 teaspoon pepper
- 1/2 cup chopped pecans, optional

In a large bowl, combine the first eight ingredients. In a small bowl, combine cranberry juice, vinegar, oil, basil, sugar, salt if desired and pepper; mix well. Pour over rice mixture and toss to coat. Refrigerate overnight. Just before serving, stir in pecans if desired. **Yield:** 12 servings.

Nutritional Analysis: One 1/2-cup serving (prepared without salt and pecans, and with rice that was cooked in unsalted water) equals 114 calories, 18 mg sodium, 0 cholesterol, 24 gm carbohydrate, 3 gm protein, 1 gm fat. **Diabetic Exchanges:** 1 starch, 1 vegetable.

Asparagus Tomato Salad

(Pictured above)

Darlene Greulich, Cambridge, Ontario

This is my husband's favorite asparagus recipe. All of our children love it, too.

 Uses less fat, sugar or salt. Includes Nutritional Analysis and Diabetic Exchanges.

- 1 pound fresh asparagus, cut into 1-inch pieces
- 4 medium tomatoes, cut into wedges
- 3 cups sliced fresh mushrooms
- 1 medium green pepper, julienned
- 1/4 cup vegetable oil
- 2 tablespoons cider vinegar
- 1 garlic clove, minced
- 1 teaspoon dried tarragon
- 3/4 teaspoon salt, optional
- 1/4 teaspoon pepper
- 1/4 teaspoon hot pepper sauce

Cook asparagus in a small amount of water until crisp-tender, about 3-4 minutes; drain and rinse with cold water. Place in a large bowl; add the tomatoes, mushrooms and green pepper. In a small bowl, combine remaining ingredients; mix well. Pour over vegetable mixture; toss to coat. Cover and refrigerate for 2 hours or overnight. **Yield:** 14 servings.

Nutritional Analysis: One 1/2-cup serving (prepared without salt) equals 55 calories, 5 mg sodium, 0 cholesterol, 1 gm carbohydrate, 4 gm protein, 4 gm fat. **Diabetic Exchanges:** 1 fat, 1/2 vegetable.

Company Fruit Salad

(Pictured below)

Connie Osterhout, Napoleon, Ohio

We first tried a salad like this at a local deli. Since I couldn't get that recipe, I starting mixing up different dressings until I hit on this one. Now I make this refreshing delightful salad for every picnic and get-together. It can be a snack, side dish or dessert.

    4 medium Golden Delicious apples, diced
    4 medium Red Delicious apples, diced
    2 cups seedless green grapes, halved
    2 cups seedless red grapes, halved
    1 can (20 ounces) pineapple chunks, drained
    1 can (11 ounces) mandarin oranges, drained
DRESSING:
    1 package (3 ounces) cream cheese, softened
    1/2 cup sour cream
    1/2 cup mayonnaise
    1/2 cup sugar

Combine all the fruit in a large bowl. In a mixing bowl, beat dressing ingredients until smooth. Pour over fruit; toss gently to coat. Serve immediately. **Yield:** 16-20 servings.

Pasta Salad with Poppy Seed Dressing

Susie Eckert, Acworth, Georgia

This pasta salad is frequently requested at family get-togethers. The poppy seed dressing is also delicious in coleslaw or with a tossed salad.

    1 package (16 ounces) bow tie *or* small tube pasta
    1 cup (4 ounces) shredded cheddar cheese
    2 cups broccoli florets
    1 cup sliced carrots
    1 cup diced cucumber
    1 cup halved cherry tomatoes
    1/2 cup chopped green onions

DRESSING:
    1/2 cup cider vinegar
    1/2 cup sugar
    1 garlic clove, minced
    1 green onion, chopped
    1/2 teaspoon ground mustard
    1/2 teaspoon salt
    1 cup vegetable oil
    4 teaspoons poppy seeds

Cook pasta according to package directions; drain and rinse with cold water. Place in a large bowl; add cheese, broccoli, carrots, cucumber, tomatoes and onions.

In a blender, combine vinegar, sugar, garlic, onion, mustard and salt; gradually add oil, blending until smooth. Add poppy seeds. Pour over pasta mixture and toss. Cover and refrigerate for at least 1 hour. **Yield:** 16-18 servings.

Roast Beef Pasta Salad

Sandy Shields, Mead, Washington

I made this salad one year when a neighbor came over to help my husband put up hay. They both were hot and dusty, so this cool dish was well received.

    1 package (16 ounces) spiral pasta
    2 cups julienned cooked roast beef
    1 cup chopped green pepper
    1 cup sliced celery
    3/4 cup chopped red onion
    1/2 cup chopped sweet red pepper
    1/3 cup chopped dill pickle
    2 to 3 green onions, sliced
DRESSING:
    2 tablespoons beef bouillon granules
    1/4 cup boiling water
    1/2 cup milk
    2 cups mayonnaise
    1 cup (8 ounces) sour cream
    1 teaspoon dill weed
Dash pepper

Cook the pasta according to package directions; drain and rinse in cold water. Place in a large bowl; add beef, green pepper, celery, onion, red pepper, pickle and green onions. For dressing, dissolve bouillon in water. Add milk, mayonnaise, sour cream, dill and pepper; mix well. Toss with pasta mixture. Cover and refrigerate until serving. **Yield:** 12-16 servings.

Picnic Slaw

Jesse and Anne Foust, Bluefield, West Virginia

Everyone loves this festive, colorful coleslaw. It not only looks good, it tastes great, too. Crisp vegetables covered with a light creamy dressing make a refreshing side dish you'll be proud to serve.

    1 medium head cabbage, shredded
    1 large carrot, shredded
    1 medium green pepper, julienned

1 medium sweet red pepper, julienned
1 medium onion, finely chopped
1/3 cup sliced green onions
1/4 cup chopped fresh parsley
DRESSING:
1/4 cup milk
1/4 cup buttermilk
1/2 cup mayonnaise
1/3 cup sugar
2 tablespoons lemon juice
1 tablespoon vinegar
1/2 teaspoon salt
1/2 teaspoon celery seed
Dash pepper

In a large bowl, combine the first seven ingredients. Combine dressing ingredients in a blender; process until smooth. Pour over vegetables; toss to coat. Cover and refrigerate overnight. Stir before serving. **Yield:** 12-16 servings.

1 medium green pepper, chopped
1 medium onion, chopped
2 cups tortilla chips, coarsely crushed, *divided*

Place beans in a Dutch oven or soup kettle; add water to cover by 2 in. Bring to a boil; boil for 2 minutes. Remove from the heat; cover and let stand for 1 hour. Drain and discard liquid. Add water to cover beans by 2 in. Bring to a boil. Reduce heat; cover and simmer for 1 to 1-1/2 hours or until tender. Rinse, drain and set aside.

For dressing, in a saucepan, combine the vinegar, oil, ketchup, brown sugar, mustard, Worcestershire sauce, chili powder, cumin, salt, pepper and hot pepper sauce. Bring to a boil. Reduce heat; cover and simmer for 10 minutes. Cool slightly. In a large salad bowl, combine the beans, corn, peppers and onion. Just before serving, stir in dressing and half of the chips. Sprinkle with remaining chips. **Yield:** 14-16 servings.

Barbecue Bean Salad

(Pictured below)

Judith Saeugling, Dubuque, Iowa

I love to cook and try new recipes. This one's a favorite. I've been collecting cookbooks for years and have picked up some very old cookbooks at estate sales.

1 pound dry pinto beans
1/4 cup cider vinegar
1/4 cup vegetable oil
1/4 cup ketchup
1/4 cup packed brown sugar
1 tablespoon Dijon mustard
1 tablespoon Worcestershire sauce
2 teaspoons chili powder
3/4 teaspoon ground cumin
1 teaspoon salt
1/4 teaspoon pepper
1/4 teaspoon hot pepper sauce
1 can (15-1/4 ounces) whole kernel corn, drained
1 medium sweet red pepper, chopped

Classic Cobb Salad

(Pictured above)

Patty Kile, Greentown, Pennsylvania

Not only is my salad's fresh flavor great—making it is a lot like putting in a garden. That's because I "plant" everything in nice, neat sections, just like I do in my vegetable garden.

6 cups torn lettuce
2 medium tomatoes, chopped
1 avocado, chopped
3/4 cup diced fully cooked ham
2 hard-cooked eggs, chopped
3/4 cup diced cooked turkey
1-1/4 cups sliced fresh mushrooms
1/2 cup crumbled blue cheese
Red onion rings, lemon wedges and sliced ripe olives, optional
Salad dressing of your choice

Arrange lettuce in a large bowl. Place tomatoes across the center, dividing the bowl in half. On one half, arrange the avocado, ham and eggs in sections. On the other half, arrange the turkey, mushrooms and blue cheese. Garnish with onion, lemon and olives if desired. Serve with salad dressing. **Yield:** 12-14 servings.

Side Dishes

Spicy Rice Pilaf (p. 29)

Chapter 3

Garden Casserole

(Pictured above)

Phyllis Hickey, Bedford, New Hampshire

I make this delicious cheesy casserole with the bounty from my vegetable garden.

>   2 pounds eggplant, peeled
>   5 teaspoons salt, *divided*
>   1/4 cup olive *or* vegetable oil
>   2 medium onions, finely chopped
>   2 garlic cloves, minced
>   2 medium zucchini, sliced 1/2 inch thick
>   5 medium tomatoes, peeled and chopped
>   2 celery ribs, sliced
>   1/4 cup minced fresh parsley
>   1/4 cup minced fresh basil
>   1/2 teaspoon pepper
>   1/2 cup grated Romano cheese
>   1 cup dry Italian bread crumbs
>   2 tablespoons butter *or* margarine, melted
>   1 cup (4 ounces) shredded mozzarella cheese

Cut eggplant into 1/2-in.-thick slices; sprinkle both sides with 3 teaspoons salt. Place in a deep dish; cover and let stand for 30 minutes. Rinse with cold water; drain and dry on paper towels. Cut into 1/2-in. cubes and saute in oil until lightly browned, about 5 minutes.

Add onions, garlic and zucchini; cook 3 minutes. Add tomatoes, celery, parsley, basil, pepper and remaining salt; bring to a boil. Reduce heat; cover and simmer for 10 minutes. Remove from the heat; stir in Romano cheese. Pour into a greased 13-in. x 9-in. x 2-in. baking dish. Combine crumbs and butter; sprinkle on top. Bake, uncovered, at 375° for 15 minutes. Sprinkle with mozzarella cheese. Return to the oven for 5 minutes or until cheese is melted. **Yield:** 12 servings.

Broccoli-Cheddar Casserole

Carol Strickland, Yuma, Arizona

We're lucky to have fresh fruits and vegetables year-round. I put bountiful Arizona broccoli to great use in this rich side dish. Even those who don't care for broccoli finish off big helpings.

>   8 cups chopped fresh broccoli
>   1 cup finely chopped onion
>   3/4 cup butter *or* margarine
>   12 eggs
>   2 cups whipping cream
>   2 cups (8 ounces) shredded cheddar cheese,
>   *divided*
>   2 teaspoons salt
>   1 teaspoon pepper

In a skillet over medium heat, saute broccoli and onion in butter until crisp-tender, about 5 minutes; set aside. In a bowl, beat eggs. Add cream and 1-3/4 cups of cheese; mix well. Stir in the broccoli mixture, salt and pepper. Pour into a greased 3-qt. baking dish; set in a larger pan filled with 1 in. of hot water.

Bake, uncovered, at 350° for 45-50 minutes or until a knife inserted near the center comes out clean. Sprinkle with remaining cheese. Let stand 10 minutes before serving. **Yield:** 12-16 servings.

Mexican Corn Casserole

Laura Kadlec, Maiden Rock, Wisconsin

This satisfying side dish resembles an old-fashioned spoon bread with zip. My family and friends agree this recipe really dresses up plain corn. It's a convenient dish to transport to a potluck.

>   4 eggs
>   1 can (15-1/4 ounces) whole kernel corn, drained
>   1 can (14-3/4 ounces) cream-style corn
>   1-1/2 cups cornmeal
>   1-1/4 cups buttermilk
>   1 cup butter *or* margarine, melted
>   2 cans (4 ounces *each*) chopped green chilies
>   2 medium onions, chopped
>   1 teaspoon baking soda
>   3 cups (12 ounces) shredded cheddar cheese,
>   *divided*
> Jalapeno pepper and sweet red pepper rings,
>   optional

Beat eggs in a large bowl; add the corn, cornmeal, buttermilk, butter, chilies, onions and baking soda; mix well. Stir in 2 cups cheese. Pour into a greased 13-in. x 9-in. x 2-in. baking dish. Bake, uncovered, at 325° for 1 hour. Top with remaining cheese. Let stand for 15 minutes before serving. Garnish with peppers if desired. **Yield:** 12-15 servings.

Creamy Herbed Vegetables

Keri Scofield Lawson, Fullerton, California

We always pass this dish to Dad first, since he likes the creamy herbed combination so much. He rates it tops among all the trimmings served for the turkey dinner when our gang gathers to celebrate Thanksgiving.

1/4 cup butter *or* margarine
1/4 cup all-purpose flour
  2 cups half-and-half cream
1/4 cup chicken broth
1/2 teaspoon *each* rubbed sage, dried thyme,
    parsley flakes, garlic powder, salt and pepper
1/2 teaspoon dried rosemary, crushed
  1 jar (16 ounces) pearl onions, drained
  1 package (16 ounces) frozen peas
  1 package (14 ounces) frozen baby carrots

Melt butter in a large saucepan; stir in flour until smooth. Gradually add cream, broth and seasonings. Bring to a boil, stirring constantly until thickened and bubbly. Add onions, peas and carrots. Cover and simmer for 30 minutes, stirring occasionally. **Yield:** 12-14 servings.

Make-Ahead Potatoes

(Pictured below)

Margaret Twitched, Danbury, Iowa

There's no need to slave away making mashed potatoes at the last minute, not when this creamy, comforting potato side dish is so handy to prepare well in advance. Plus, it's an easy dish for people to serve themselves and it looks so appealing on a buffet.

10 large potatoes, peeled and quartered
  1 cup (8 ounces) sour cream
  1 package (8 ounces) cream cheese, softened
  6 tablespoons butter *or* margarine, *divided*
  2 tablespoons dried minced onion
1/2 to 1 teaspoon salt
Paprika

Place potatoes in a Dutch oven or large kettle; cover with water and bring to a boil. Reduce heat; cover and cook for 20-25 minutes or until potatoes are tender. Drain and place in a bowl; mash. Add sour cream, cream cheese, 4 tablespoons butter, onion and salt; stir until smooth and the cream cheese and butter are

melted. Spread in a greased 13-in. x 9-in. x 2-in. baking dish. Melt remaining butter; drizzle over potatoes. Sprinkle with paprika.

Cover and refrigerate 8 hours or overnight. Remove from the refrigerator 30 minutes before baking. Cover and bake at 350° for 40 minutes; uncover and bake 20 minutes longer. **Yield:** 12 servings.

Three-Bean Baked Beans

(Pictured above)

Julie Currington, Gahanna, Ohio

I got this recipe from an aunt and made a couple of changes to suit our tastes. With ground beef and bacon mixed in, these satisfying beans are a big hit at backyard barbecues and church picnics. I'm always asked to bring my "special" beans.

1/2 pound ground beef
  5 bacon strips, diced
1/2 cup chopped onion
  2 cans (16 ounces *each*) pork and beans,
    undrained
  1 can (16 ounces) butter beans, rinsed and
    drained
  1 can (16 ounces) kidney beans, rinsed and
    drained
1/3 cup packed brown sugar
1/4 cup sugar
1/4 cup ketchup
1/4 cup barbecue sauce
  2 tablespoons molasses
  2 tablespoons prepared mustard
1/2 teaspoon chili powder
1/2 teaspoon salt

In a large skillet or saucepan over medium heat, brown beef, bacon and onion; drain. Add beans. Combine remaining ingredients; stir into bean mixture. Pour into a greased 2-1/2-qt. baking dish. Bake, uncovered, at 350° for 1 hour or until beans reach the desired thickness. **Yield:** 12 servings.

Au Gratin Potatoes

Carol Van Sickle, Versailles, Kentucky

Au gratin potatoes are real comfort food with their creamy cheese sauce. They're easier to serve a crowd than regular mashed potatoes.

8 cups cubed peeled potatoes
1/4 cup butter *or* margarine
2 tablespoons all-purpose flour
3/4 teaspoon salt
1/8 teaspoon pepper
1-1/2 cups milk
1 pound process American cheese, cubed
Minced fresh parsley

In a large saucepan, cook potatoes in boiling water until tender. Drain and place in a greased 2-1/2-qt. baking dish. In a saucepan, melt butter. Add the flour, salt and pepper; stir to form a smooth paste. Gradually add milk, stirring constantly. Bring to a boil; boil and stir for 1 minute. Add cheese; stir just until melted. Pour over potatoes. Cover and bake at 350° for 45-50 minutes or until bubbly. Sprinkle with parsley. **Yield:** 12 servings.

Old-Fashioned Baked Beans

(Pictured below)

Jesse and Anne Foust, Bluefield, West Virginia

These hearty beans are a super side dish for a casual meal. The ingredients blend perfectly for a wonderful from-scratch taste. The old-fashioned flavor will have people standing in line for more.

1 pound dry navy beans
1-1/2 teaspoons salt
4 quarts cold water, *divided*
1 cup chopped red onion
1/2 cup molasses
6 bacon strips, cooked and crumbled

1/4 cup packed brown sugar
1 teaspoon ground mustard
1/4 teaspoon pepper

In a large saucepan or Dutch oven, bring beans, salt and 2 qts. water to a boil; boil for 2 minutes. Remove from the heat; let stand for 1 hour. Drain beans and discard liquid. Return beans to pan. Cover with remaining water; bring to a boil. Reduce heat; cover and simmer for 1-1/2 to 2 hours or until beans are tender. Drain, reserving liquid.

In a greased 2-1/2-qt. baking dish, combine beans, 1 cup liquid, onion, molasses, bacon, brown sugar, mustard and pepper. Cover and bake at 325° for 3 to 3-1/2 hours or until beans have reached desired thickness, stirring occasionally. Add more of the reserved cooking liquid if needed. **Yield:** 12-16 servings.

Spinach Dumplings

Gail Sykora, Menomonee Falls, Wisconsin

I've been making these green dumplings—"gnocchi verdi" in Italian—since the 1970s. They're a great side dish for most any meal.

1 tablespoon finely chopped onion
6 tablespoons butter *or* margarine
3 packages (10 ounces *each*) frozen chopped spinach, thawed and well drained
1 cup ricotta cheese
1-1/2 cups all-purpose flour, *divided*
1/2 cup grated Parmesan cheese
3/4 teaspoon garlic salt
2 eggs, beaten
3 quarts water
3 tablespoons chicken bouillon granules
TOPPING:
1/4 cup butter *or* margarine, melted
1/2 cup grated Parmesan cheese

In a skillet, saute onion in butter until tender. Add spinach; cook and stir over medium heat until the liquid has evaporated, about 5 minutes. Stir in ricotta; cook and stir for 3 minutes. Transfer to a large bowl. Add 3/4 cup of flour, Parmesan cheese and garlic salt. Cool for 5 minutes. Stir in eggs; mix well.

Place remaining flour in a bowl. Drop batter by tablespoonfuls into flour; roll gently to coat and shape each into an oval. In a large saucepan, bring water and bouillon to a boil; reduce heat. Add a third of the dumplings at a time; simmer, uncovered, for 8-10 minutes or until a toothpick inserted into a dumpling comes out clean. Remove with a slotted spoon; keep warm. Drizzle with butter; sprinkle with Parmesan. **Yield:** 12 servings.

Hash Brown Casserole

Susan Auten, Douglasville, Georgia

People always go back for seconds whenever I serve these rich, cheesy potatoes. This comforting casserole is a snap to fix using quick convenient packaged ingredients. It travels well to potlucks and other parties, too.

- 2 cans (10-3/4 ounces *each*) condensed cream of potato soup, undiluted
- 1 cup (8 ounces) sour cream
- 1/2 teaspoon garlic salt
- 1 package (2 pounds) frozen hash brown potatoes
- 2 cups (8 ounces) shredded cheddar cheese
- 1/2 cup grated Parmesan cheese

In a large bowl, combine the soup, sour cream and garlic salt. Add potatoes and cheddar cheese; mix well. Pour into a greased 13-in. x 9-in. x 2-in. baking dish. Top with Parmesan cheese. Bake, uncovered, at 350° for 55-60 minutes or until potatoes are tender. **Yield:** 12-16 servings.

Spicy Rice Pilaf

(Pictured below)

Cynthia Gobeli, Norton, Ohio

I found this side dish recipe back in the 1950s and have made some minor adjustments to it over the years to update the flavor. In summer, I like to serve the pilaf over slices of red ripe tomatoes. It's just as good all by itself as well.

- 1/2 cup chopped onion
- 2 tablespoons olive *or* vegetable oil
- 2 cups chicken broth
- 1/4 cup lentils, rinsed
- 1 can (16 ounces) kidney beans, rinsed and drained
- 1 cup salsa
- 1 cup uncooked long grain rice
- 1 cup frozen corn
- 1 jar (2 ounces) diced pimientos, drained
- 1 teaspoon chili powder

In a saucepan over medium heat, saute onion in oil until tender. Add broth and lentils; bring to a boil. Reduce heat; cover and simmer for 15 minutes. Stir in remaining ingredients; bring to a boil. Reduce heat; cover and simmer 20-25 minutes longer or until lentils and rice are tender. **Yield:** 12 servings.

Mushroom Green Bean Casserole

(Pictured above)

Pat Richter, Lake Placid, Florida

Most traditional green bean casseroles center around mushroom soup and french-fried onions. This from-scratch variation features fresh mushrooms, sliced water chestnuts and slivered almonds.

- 1 pound fresh mushrooms, sliced
- 1 large onion, chopped
- 1/2 cup butter *or* margarine
- 1/4 cup all-purpose flour
- 1 cup half-and-half cream
- 1 jar (16 ounces) process cheese sauce
- 2 teaspoons soy sauce
- 1/2 teaspoon pepper
- 1/8 teaspoon hot pepper sauce
- 1 can (8 ounces) sliced water chestnuts, drained
- 2 packages (16 ounces *each*) frozen French-style green beans, thawed and well drained

Slivered almonds

In a skillet, saute mushrooms and onion in butter until tender. Stir in flour until blended. Gradually stir in cream. Bring to a boil; cook and stir for 2 minutes. Stir in cheese sauce, soy sauce, pepper and hot pepper sauce until cheese is melted. Remove from heat; stir in water chestnuts. Place beans in an ungreased 3-qt. baking dish. Pour cheese mixture over top. Sprinkle with almonds. Bake, uncovered, at 375° for 25-30 minutes or until bubbly. **Yield:** 14-16 servings.

Vegetable Noodle Casserole

(Pictured at right)

Jeanette Hios, Brooklyn, New York

If you're looking for a filling side dish, this recipe fits the bill. It combines nutritious vegetables and hearty noodles in a delectable cream sauce. Whenever I serve this dish, it gets passed around until the pan is scraped completely clean.

    1 can (10-3/4 ounces) condensed cream of chicken soup, undiluted
    1 can (10-3/4 ounces) condensed cream of broccoli soup, undiluted
1-1/2 cups milk
    1 cup grated Parmesan cheese, *divided*
    3 garlic cloves, minced
    2 tablespoons dried parsley flakes
    1/2 teaspoon pepper
    1/4 teaspoon salt
    1 package (16 ounces) wide egg noodles, cooked and drained
    1 package (16 ounces) frozen broccoli, cauliflower and carrot blend, thawed
    2 cups frozen corn, thawed

In a bowl, combine soups, milk, 3/4 cup Parmesan cheese, garlic, parsley, pepper and salt; mix well. Add noodles and vegetables; mix well. Pour into a greased 13-in. x 9-in. x 2-in. baking dish. Sprinkle with the remaining Parmesan. Cover and bake at 350° for 45-50 minutes or until heated through. **Yield:** 12-14 servings.

Mushroom Wild Rice

(Pictured below)

Charlene Baert, Winnipeg, Manitoba

This colorful casserole is a standout from my mother's collection of family Thanksgiving recipes. Excellent texture and taste guarantee it won't play second fiddle to either the turkey or the pumpkin pie!

    4 cups water
    1 cup uncooked wild rice
    1 teaspoon butter *or* margarine
1-1/2 teaspoons salt, *divided*
    1/2 cup uncooked brown rice
    8 bacon strips, diced
    2 cups sliced fresh mushrooms
    1 large onion, chopped
    1 medium green pepper, chopped
    1 medium sweet red pepper, chopped
    1 celery rib, thinly sliced
    1 can (14-1/2 ounces) beef broth
    2 tablespoons cornstarch
    1/4 cup cold water
    1/2 cup slivered almonds

In a large saucepan, bring water, wild rice, butter and 1/2 teaspoon salt to a boil. Reduce heat; cover and simmer for 40 minutes. Stir in brown rice. Cover and simmer 25-30 minutes longer or until rice is tender.

Meanwhile, in a large skillet, cook bacon until crisp. Remove bacon to paper towels; drain, reserving 2 tablespoons drippings. In the drippings, saute mushrooms, onion, peppers and celery until tender. Stir in broth and remaining salt. Bring to a boil. Combine the cornstarch and cold water until smooth; stir into the mushroom mixture. Cook and stir for 2 minutes or until thickened and bubbly; stir in almonds and bacon.

Drain rice; add mushroom mixture. Transfer to a greased 13-in. x 9-in. x 2-in. baking dish. Cover and bake at 350° for 25 minutes. Uncover; bake 5-10 minutes longer or until heated through. **Yield:** 12 servings.

Oven-Fried Potatoes

Delores Billings, Koksilah, British Columbia

These tasty potatoes are a family favorite. They're easy to make and travel well to potlucks. We enjoy them as part of a hearty breakfast or alongside various meats for supper.

   12 medium potatoes, peeled and cubed
   1/4 cup grated Parmesan cheese
   2 teaspoons salt

1 teaspoon garlic powder
1 teaspoon paprika
1/2 teaspoon pepper
1/3 cup vegetable oil

Place potatoes in two large resealable plastic bags. Combine the Parmesan cheese and seasonings; add to potatoes and shake to coat. Pour oil into two 15-in. x 10-in. x 1-in. baking pans; pour potatoes into pans. Bake, uncovered, at 375° for 40-50 minutes or until tender. **Yield:** 12-14 servings.

Creamy Squash Casserole

Sue Moore, Columbiana, Ohio

This casserole is so easy to prepare. With squash, carrots and stuffing, it's a super side dish to take to harvesttime and holiday dinners.

2 pounds acorn *or* butternut squash
1 can (10-3/4 ounces) condensed cream of
    chicken soup, undiluted
1 cup (8 ounces) sour cream
1/3 cup butter *or* margarine, melted
2 medium carrots, shredded
1/2 cup finely chopped onion
2-1/4 cups herb-seasoned stuffing mix, *divided*

Cut squash in half; remove and discard peel and seeds. Cut squash into 1/2-in. cubes. Cook squash in a small amount of water for 3 minutes; drain and set aside. In a bowl, combine soup, sour cream, butter, carrots and onion; stir in 2 cups of stuffing mix. Fold in squash.

Transfer to a greased 11-in. x 7-in. x 2-in. baking dish. Sprinkle with remaining stuffing mix. Bake, uncovered, at 350° for 25 minutes or until squash is tender. **Yield:** 12 servings.

Mushroom Stuffing

Kathy Traetow, Waverly, Iowa

I first tried this stuffing a few years ago, and it fast became our family's favorite. My hearty corn bread mixture is flavored with mushrooms and bacon.

4 bacon strips, diced
4 celery ribs, chopped
1 medium onion, chopped
1 pound fresh mushrooms, chopped
1 teaspoon rubbed sage
1/2 teaspoon salt
1/4 teaspoon pepper
1 package (16 ounces) corn bread stuffing
1/2 cup chopped celery leaves
2 tablespoons minced fresh parsley
4 eggs, beaten
2-1/2 cups chicken broth
1 tablespoon butter *or* margarine

In a large skillet, cook bacon until crisp; remove with a slotted spoon to paper towel. Drain, reserving 2 table-spoons of drippings. Saute celery and onion in drippings

until tender. Add mushrooms, sage, salt and pepper; cook and stir for 5 minutes. Remove from the heat; stir in stuffing, celery leaves, parsley and bacon; mix well.

Combine eggs and broth. Add to stuffing mixture and mix well. Spread in a greased 13-in. x 9-in. x 2-in. baking dish (dish will be full). Dot with butter. Cover and bake at 350° for 30 minutes. Uncover and bake 10 minutes longer or until lightly browned. **Yield:** 13 cups.

Editor's Note: Stuffing may be baked in one 16- to 18-pound turkey or three 5- to 7-pound roasting chickens.

Four-Cheese Macaroni

(Pictured below)

Darlene Marturano, West Suffield, Connecticut

I adapted this recipe from one a friend gave to me. It has a distinctive blue cheese taste and is very filling. I like to serve it with chicken.

1 package (16 ounces) elbow macaroni
1/4 cup butter *or* margarine
1/4 cup all-purpose flour
1/2 teaspoon salt
1/8 teaspoon pepper
3 cups milk
2 cups (8 ounces) shredded cheddar cheese
1-1/2 cups (6 ounces) shredded Swiss cheese
1/2 cup crumbled blue cheese
1/2 cup grated Parmesan cheese

Cook macaroni according to package directions. Meanwhile, in a 5-qt. Dutch oven over medium heat, melt butter. Stir in flour, salt and pepper until smooth. Bring to a boil; boil and stir for 2 minutes. Gradually add milk, stirring constantly. Reduce heat to low; add cheeses and stir until melted. Drain macaroni; add to cheese sauce and stir until well coated. **Yield:** 12 servings.

Artichoke Spinach Casserole

(Pictured above)

Judy Johnson, Missoula, Montana

Although he isn't a fan of spinach, my husband loves this dish. The combination of ingredients may sound unusual, but the flavors meld well. It's an excellent side vegetable for a formal dinner.

- 1 pound fresh mushrooms, sliced
- 1/3 cup chicken broth
- 1 tablespoon all-purpose flour
- 1/2 cup evaporated milk
- 4 packages (10 ounces *each*) frozen chopped spinach, thawed and well drained
- 2 cans (14-1/2 ounces *each*) diced tomatoes, drained
- 2 cans (14 ounces *each*) water-packed artichoke hearts, drained and thinly sliced
- 1 cup (8 ounces) sour cream
- 1/2 cup mayonnaise
- 3 tablespoons lemon juice
- 1/2 teaspoon garlic powder
- 1/4 teaspoon salt
- 1/4 teaspoon pepper

Paprika, optional

In a large skillet, cook mushrooms and broth over medium heat until tender, about 3 minutes. Remove mushrooms with a slotted spoon and set aside. Whisk flour and milk until smooth; add to skillet. Bring to a boil; cook and stir for 2 minutes. Remove from the heat; stir in spinach, tomatoes and mushrooms.

Place half of the artichokes in an ungreased 13-in. x 9-in. x 2-in. baking dish. Top with half of the spinach mixture. Repeat layers. Combine the sour cream, mayonnaise, lemon juice, garlic powder, salt and pepper; dollop over the top of the casserole. Sprinkle with paprika if desired. Bake, uncovered, at 350° for 25-30 minutes or until bubbly. **Yield:** 12-14 servings.

End-of-Summer Vegetable Bake

(Pictured below)

Judy Williams, Hayden, Idaho

When my husband worked as a deputy ag commissioner, he'd bring me bushels of vegetables from area farms. This pretty side dish is the result—it's easy to fix but impressive enough for company.

- 1 small head cauliflower, broken into small florets (about 5 cups)
- 1 medium bunch broccoli, cut into small florets (about 4 cups)
- 1 medium onion, chopped
- 2 garlic cloves, minced
- 1 tablespoon butter *or* margarine
- 2 medium tomatoes, chopped
- 3/4 teaspoon dried basil
- 3/4 teaspoon dried oregano
- 3/4 teaspoon salt
- 1/4 teaspoon pepper
- 1/4 teaspoon hot pepper sauce
- 4 eggs
- 1/3 cup half-and-half cream
- 1-1/2 cups (6 ounces) shredded Swiss cheese, *divided*
- 1/4 cup shredded Parmesan cheese

Place the cauliflower and broccoli in a saucepan with a small amount of water. Bring to a boil. Reduce heat; cover and simmer for 5-10 minutes or until crisp-tender. Drain and set aside.

In a large skillet, saute onion and garlic in butter until tender. Stir in tomatoes, seasonings, cauliflower and broccoli. Cook, uncovered, until heated through, about 4 minutes, stirring occasionally. Remove from the heat and set aside.

In a large bowl, beat eggs and cream; stir in 1 cup Swiss cheese, Parmesan cheese and the vegetable mixture. Transfer to a greased shallow 2-qt. baking dish. Sprinkle with remaining Swiss cheese. Bake, uncovered, at 375° for 25-30 minutes or until a knife inserted near the center comes out clean. Let stand 10 minutes before serving. **Yield:** 12 servings.

Corn Stuffing Balls

Audrey Groe, Lake Mills, Iowa

My mom had many "winning" recipes, and this was one of our family's favorites. I can still picture these stuffing balls encircling the large meat platter piled high with one of her delicious entrees.

        6 cups herb-seasoned stuffing croutons
        1 cup chopped celery
    1/2 cup chopped onion
    3/4 cup butter *or* margarine, *divided*
        1 can (14-3/4 ounces) cream-style corn
        1 cup water
    1-1/2 teaspoons poultry seasoning
    3/4 teaspoon salt
    1/4 teaspoon pepper
        3 egg yolks, beaten

Place croutons in a large bowl and set aside. In a skillet, saute celery and onion in 1/2 cup butter. Add the corn, water, poultry seasoning, salt and pepper; bring to a boil. Remove from the heat; cool for 5 minutes. Pour over croutons. Add egg yolks and mix gently.

Shape 1/2 cupfuls into balls; flatten slightly. Place in a greased 15-in. x 10-in. x 1-in. baking pan. Melt remaining butter; drizzle over balls. Bake, uncovered, at 375° for 30 minutes or until lightly browned. **Yield:** 12 servings.

Country Pineapple Casserole

Margaret Lindemann, Kenvil, New Jersey

My family enjoyed this dish at a church supper, so I asked for the recipe. I've made it for many covered-dish meals since and have received compliments.

    1/2 cup butter *or* margarine, softened
        2 cups sugar
        8 eggs
        2 cans (20 ounces *each*) crushed pineapple, drained
        3 tablespoons lemon juice
    10 slices day-old white bread, cubed

In a mixing bowl, cream butter and sugar. Add the eggs, one at a time, beating well after each addition. Stir in pineapple and lemon juice. Fold in the bread cubes. Pour into a greased 13-in. x 9-in. x 2-in. baking dish. Bake, uncovered, at 325° for 35-40 minutes or until set. **Yield:** 12-16 servings.

Almond-Topped Carrots

Karen Regennitter, Ritzville, Washington

Here's a different way to cook carrots. It's a nice addition to a fancy meal and jazzes up an everyday dinner.

        2 pounds carrots, julienned
        2 cups water
    1/2 cup golden raisins
    1/2 cup butter *or* margarine, melted
        6 tablespoons honey
        2 tablespoons lemon juice
    1/2 teaspoon ground ginger
    Dash pepper
    1/2 cup slivered almonds, toasted

In a saucepan, bring carrots and water to a boil. Reduce heat. Cover and cook for 10 minutes or until crisp-tender; drain. Add the raisins, butter, honey, lemon juice, ginger and pepper. Place in a greased 2-qt. baking dish. Cover and bake at 350° for 35 minutes or until the carrots are tender. Sprinkle with almonds before serving. **Yield:** 12 servings.

Twice-Baked Sweet Potatoes

(Pictured above)

Miriam Christophel, Battle Creek, Michigan

When I prepare these sweet potatoes, I like to serve them with ham. Those two different tastes always team really well.

        6 large sweet potatoes (3-1/2 to 4 pounds)
    1/4 cup orange juice
        6 tablespoons cold butter *or* margarine, *divided*
    1/4 cup all-purpose flour
    1/4 cup packed brown sugar
    1/4 teaspoon ground cinnamon
    1/4 teaspoon ground ginger
    1/8 teaspoon ground mace
    1/4 cup chopped pecans

Pierce potatoes with a fork. Bake at 375° for 40-60 minutes or until tender. Allow potatoes to cool to the touch. Cut them in half lengthwise; carefully scoop out pulp, leaving a 1/4-in. shell. Place pulp in a large bowl. Add orange juice. Melt 3 tablespoons butter; add to pulp and beat until smooth. Stuff the potato shells; place in an ungreased 15-in. x 10-in. x 1-in. baking pan.

In a small bowl, combine flour, brown sugar, cinnamon, ginger and mace. Cut in remaining butter until crumbly. Stir in pecans. Sprinkle over potatoes. Bake at 350° for 20-25 minutes or until golden and heated through. **Yield:** 12 servings.

Soups & Sandwiches

Three-Meat Stromboli (p. 45)

Chapter 4

"Bring an Ingredient" Soup

(Pictured above)

Mary Anne McWhirter, Pearland, Texas

A steaming bowl of soup is just the thing to take the chill off a cold winter evening spent caroling. Asking each guest to bring an ingredient adds to the fun.

>   4 cups thinly sliced onions
>   1 garlic clove, minced
>   3 tablespoons butter *or* margarine
>   3 tablespoons all-purpose flour
>   6 cans (14-1/2 ounces *each*) beef broth
>   2 cups tomato puree
>   1 tablespoon red wine vinegar *or* cider vinegar
>   1 tablespoon Worcestershire sauce
>   1 tablespoon sugar
>   1/2 teaspoon *each* dried oregano, tarragon,
>   ground cumin, salt and pepper
>   1/4 to 1/2 teaspoon hot pepper sauce
> VEGETABLES (choose two *or* three):
> 1-1/2 cups *each* diced green pepper, tomato *or*
>   carrots
>   2 cups sliced fresh mushrooms
> MEATS (choose two):
>   3 cups cooked mini meatballs
>   3 cups cubed cooked chicken
>   3 cups diced fully cooked ham
>   1 package (10 ounces) smoked kielbasa,
>   sliced and browned
> GARNISHES (choose three *or* four):
> Shredded cheddar cheese, garbanzo beans, sour
>   cream, chopped fresh parsley, croutons *or*
>   popcorn

In a large Dutch oven, saute the onions and garlic in butter until tender. Stir in flour and blend well. Add broth, puree, vinegar and seasonings; mix well. Bring to a boil; reduce heat and simmer for 40 minutes. Add two or three vegetables; simmer for 30 minutes or until tender. Add two meats; heat through. Garnish as desired. **Yield:** 16-18 servings (4-1/2 quarts).

Lima Bean Soup

Kathleen Olsack, North Cape May, New Jersey

Each fall there's a Lima Bean Festival in nearby West Cape May to honor the many growers there and showcase different recipes using their crop. This comforting chowder was a festival recipe contest winner several years ago.

>   3 cans (14-1/2 ounces *each*) chicken broth
>   2 cans (15 ounces *each*) lima beans, rinsed and
>   drained
>   3 medium carrots, thinly sliced
>   2 medium potatoes, peeled and diced
>   2 small sweet red peppers, chopped
>   2 small onions, chopped
>   2 celery ribs, thinly sliced
>   1/4 cup butter *or* margarine
> 1-1/2 teaspoons dried marjoram
>   1/2 teaspoon salt
>   1/2 teaspoon pepper
>   1/2 teaspoon dried oregano
>   1 cup half-and-half cream
>   3 bacon strips, cooked and crumbled

In a Dutch oven or soup kettle, combine the first 12 ingredients; bring to a boil over medium heat. Reduce heat; cover and simmer for 25-35 minutes or until vegetables are tender. Add cream; heat through but do not boil. Sprinkle with bacon just before serving. **Yield:** 10-12 servings (3 quarts).

Chicken 'n' Dumpling Soup

Rachel Hinz, St. James, Minnesota

This recipe's one I had to learn to marry into my husband's family! It is the traditional Hinz Christmas Eve meal. My father was a pastor who was always too keyed up from preaching to enjoy a big Sunday dinner. So I learned to make soup early on.

>   1 broiler/fryer chicken (3 to 3-1/2 pounds)
>   3 quarts water
>   1/4 cup chicken bouillon granules
>   1 bay leaf
>   1 teaspoon whole peppercorns
>   1/8 teaspoon ground allspice
>   6 cups uncooked wide noodles
>   4 cups sliced carrots
>   1 package (10 ounces) frozen mixed vegetables
>   3/4 cup sliced celery
>   1/2 cup chopped onion
>   1/4 cup uncooked long grain rice
>   2 tablespoons minced fresh parsley
> DUMPLINGS:
> 1-1/3 cups all-purpose flour
>   2 teaspoons baking powder
>   1 teaspoon dried thyme
>   1/2 teaspoon salt
>   2/3 cup milk
>   2 tablespoons vegetable oil

In a Dutch oven or soup kettle, combine the first six ingredients; bring to a boil. Reduce heat; cover and simmer for 1-1/2 hours. Remove chicken; allow to cool. Strain broth; discard bay leaf and peppercorns. Skim fat. Debone chicken and cut into chunks; return chicken and broth to pan. Add noodles, vegetables, rice and parsley; bring to a simmer.

For dumplings, combine flour, baking powder, thyme and salt in a bowl. Combine milk and oil; stir into dry ingredients. Drop by teaspoonfuls onto simmering soup. Reduce heat; cover and simmer for 15 minutes (do not lift the cover). **Yield:** 20 servings (5 quarts).

Harvest Turkey Soup

(Pictured below)

Linda Sand, Winsted, Connecticut

The recipe for this super soup evolved over the years. I've been diabetic since I was 12, so I've learned to use herbs and spices to make dishes like this taste terrific. It also has a colorful blend of vegetables.

 Uses less fat, sugar or salt. Includes Nutritional Analysis and Diabetic Exchanges.

1 turkey carcass (from a 12-pound turkey)
5 quarts water
2 large carrots, shredded
1 cup chopped celery
1 large onion, chopped
4 chicken bouillon cubes
1 can (28 ounces) stewed tomatoes
3/4 cup fresh *or* frozen peas
3/4 cup long grain rice
1 package (10 ounces) frozen chopped spinach
1 tablespoon salt, optional
3/4 teaspoon pepper
1/2 teaspoon dried marjoram
1/2 teaspoon dried thyme

Place the turkey carcass and water in a Dutch oven or soup kettle; bring to a boil. Reduce heat; cover and simmer for 1-1/2 hours. Remove carcass; allow to cool. Remove turkey from bones and cut into bite-size pieces; set aside. Strain broth. Add carrots, celery, onion and bouillon; bring to a boil. Reduce heat; cover and simmer

for 30 minutes. Add the tomatoes, peas, rice, spinach, salt if desired, pepper, marjoram, thyme and reserved turkey. Return to a boil; cook, uncovered, for 20 minutes or until rice is tender. **Yield:** 22 servings (5-1/2 quarts).

Nutritional Analysis: One 1-cup serving (prepared with reduced-sodium bouillon and without salt) equals 289 calories, 218 mg sodium, 107 mg cholesterol, 11 gm carbohydrate, 43 gm protein, 7 gm fat. **Diabetic Exchanges:** 4 very lean meat, 1 fat, 1 starch, 1 vegetable.

Parmesan Potato Soup

(Pictured above)

Tami Walters, Kingsport, Tennessee

Even my husband, who's not much of a soup eater, likes this. With bread and a salad, it's a satisfying meal.

4 medium baking potatoes (about 2 pounds)
3/4 cup chopped onion
1/2 cup butter *or* margarine
1/2 cup all-purpose flour
1/2 teaspoon dried basil
1/2 teaspoon seasoned salt
1/4 teaspoon celery salt
1/4 teaspoon garlic powder
1/4 teaspoon onion salt
1/4 teaspoon pepper
1/4 teaspoon rubbed sage
1/4 teaspoon dried thyme
4-1/2 cups chicken broth
6 cups milk
3/4 to 1 cup grated Parmesan cheese
10 bacon strips, cooked and crumbled

Pierce potatoes with a fork; bake in the oven or microwave until tender. Cool, peel and cube; set aside. In a large Dutch oven or soup kettle over medium heat, saute onion in butter until tender. Stir in flour and seasonings. Gradually add broth, stirring constantly. Bring to a boil; cook and stir for 2 minutes. Add potatoes; return to a boil. Reduce heat; cover and simmer for 10 minutes. Add milk and cheese; heat through. Stir in bacon. **Yield:** 10-12 servings.

Louisiana Gumbo

Wilton and Gloria Mason, Springhill, Louisiana

This soup recipe certainly reflects our area of the country. It's so thick and hearty, it really is a meal in itself.

    1 broiler/fryer chicken (3 to 3-1/2 pounds), cut up
    2 quarts water
    3/4 cup all-purpose flour
    1/2 cup vegetable oil
    1/2 cup sliced green onions
    1/2 cup chopped onion
    1/2 cup chopped green pepper
    1/2 cup chopped sweet red pepper
    1/2 cup chopped celery
    2 garlic cloves, minced
    1/2 pound fully cooked smoked sausage, cut into
        1-inch cubes
    1/2 pound fully cooked ham, cut into 3/4-inch
        cubes
    1/2 pound fresh *or* frozen uncooked shrimp,
        peeled and deveined
    1 cup cut fresh *or* frozen okra (3/4-inch pieces)
    1 can (15 ounces) kidney beans, rinsed and
        drained
    1/2 teaspoon salt
    1/4 teaspoon pepper
    1/4 teaspoon hot pepper sauce
Hot cooked rice, optional

Place the chicken and water in a Dutch oven; bring to a boil. Skim fat. Reduce heat; cover and simmer 30-45 minutes or until chicken is tender. Remove chicken; cool. Reserve 6 cups broth. Remove chicken from bones; cut into bite-size pieces.

In a 4-qt. kettle, mix flour and oil until smooth; cook and stir over medium-low heat until browned, 2-3 minutes. Stir in onions, peppers, celery and garlic; cook for 5 minutes or until vegetables are tender. Stir in the sausage, ham and reserved broth and chicken; cover and simmer for 45 minutes. Add the shrimp, okra, beans, salt, pepper and hot pepper sauce; cover and simmer 10 minutes longer or until shrimp is cooked. Serve over rice if desired. **Yield:** 12 servings.

Beef Barley Soup

Sharon Kolenc, Jasper, Alberta

When making this soup, I tend to clean out the refrigerator by adding all kinds of leftovers.

    2 cups beef broth
    8 cups water
    2 cups chopped cooked roast beef
    1/2 cup chopped carrots
    3 celery ribs, chopped
    1/2 cup chopped onion
    1 can (14-1/2 ounces) diced tomatoes, undrained
    1 cup quick-cooking barley
    1 teaspoon dried oregano
    1/2 teaspoon pepper
    1 can (10-3/4 ounces) condensed tomato soup,
        undiluted

    1/2 cup frozen *or* canned peas
    1/2 cup frozen *or* canned cut green *or* wax beans
Seasoned salt to taste

In a large kettle or Dutch oven, combine the first 10 ingredients; bring to a boil. Reduce heat; cover and simmer for 25 minutes, stirring occasionally. Add soup, peas and beans. Simmer, uncovered, for 10 minutes. Add seasoned salt. **Yield:** 12-14 servings (about 3-1/2 quarts).

Chili for a Crowd

(Pictured above)

Lisa Humphreys, Wasilla, Alaska

The basis for this recipe was handed down to me by my aunt, who said she got it from a "grizzled Montana mountain man". I added some zesty ingredients to come up with the final version. Hot food is something that my husband's family isn't accustomed to. So I adjust the spices for them.

    3 pounds ground beef
    2 cans (28 ounces *each*) diced tomatoes,
        undrained
    4 cans (15 to 16 ounces *each*) kidney, pinto
        and/or black beans, rinsed and drained
    1 pound smoked kielbasa, sliced and halved
    2 large onions, halved and thinly sliced
    2 cans (8 ounces *each*) tomato sauce
    2/3 cup hickory-flavored barbecue sauce
1-1/2 cups water
    1/2 cup packed brown sugar
    5 fresh banana peppers, seeded and sliced
    2 tablespoons chili powder
    2 teaspoons ground mustard
    2 teaspoons instant coffee granules
    1 teaspoon *each* dried oregano, thyme and sage
    1/2 to 1 teaspoon cayenne pepper
    1/2 to 1 teaspoon crushed red pepper flakes
    2 garlic cloves, minced

In an 8-qt. kettle or Dutch oven, cook beef until no longer pink; drain. Add remaining ingredients; bring to a boil. Reduce heat; cover and simmer for 1 hour, stirring occasionally. **Yield:** 20-24 servings (6 quarts).

Tomato Garlic Soup

(Pictured below)

Lynn Thompson, Reston, Virginia

I like to make this soup when I'm expecting a lot of people for dinner. My guests enjoy it, too.

  10 whole garlic heads
  3/4 cup olive *or* vegetable oil
    4 cans (one 14-1/2 ounces, three 28 ounces) diced tomatoes, undrained
    1 medium onion, diced
    3 cans (14-1/2 ounces *each*) stewed tomatoes
  2/3 cup whipping cream
    1 to 3 tablespoons chopped pickled jalapeno peppers
    2 teaspoons garlic pepper
    2 teaspoons sugar
 1-1/2 teaspoons salt
Croutons and shredded Parmesan cheese, optional

Remove papery outer skin from garlic (do not peel or separate cloves). Cut tops off garlic heads; place cut side up in an ungreased 8-in. square baking dish. Pour oil over garlic. Bake, uncovered, at 375° for 45-55 minutes or until softened. Cool for 10-15 minutes.

Squeeze softened garlic into a blender or food processor. Add the 14-1/2-oz. can of diced tomatoes; cover and process until smooth. Set aside. Transfer 1/4 cup of oil from the baking dish to a Dutch oven or soup kettle (discard the remaining oil or save for another use). Saute onion in oil over medium heat until soft. Stir in the stewed tomatoes, cream, jalapenos, garlic pepper, sugar, salt, pureed tomato mixture and remaining diced

tomatoes. Bring to a boil. Reduce heat; cover and simmer for 1 hour. Garnish with croutons and cheese if desired. **Yield:** 18-20 servings (4-1/2 quarts).

Ham and Bean Chowder

(Pictured above)

Joe Ann Heavrin, Memphis, Tennessee

We also call this 2-Day Bean Chowder, since it can be started in the afternoon, chilled overnight and finished off the next day—if you can wait to taste it!

    1 pound dried great northern beans
    2 cups chopped onion
    1 cup sliced celery
    2 garlic cloves, minced
    3 tablespoons butter *or* margarine
    1 meaty ham bone
    2 cups water
    1 can (14-1/2 ounces) chicken broth
    1 can (14-1/2 ounces) stewed tomatoes
    2 bay leaves
    2 whole cloves
  1/2 teaspoon pepper
    2 cups milk
    2 cups (8 ounces) shredded cheddar cheese

Place beans in a Dutch oven or soup kettle; add water to cover by 2 in. Bring to a boil; boil for 2 minutes. Remove from the heat; cover and let stand for 1 hour. Drain beans and discard liquid. In the same kettle, saute onion, celery and garlic in butter until tender. Add beans, ham bone, water, broth, tomatoes, bay leaves, cloves and pepper; bring to a boil. Reduce heat; cover and simmer for 2 hours.

Remove ham bone, bay leaves and cloves. When cool enough to handle, remove ham from bone; cut into small pieces and return to soup. Chill for 8 hours or overnight. Skim fat from soup. Stir in milk; cook on low until heated through. Just before serving, stir in cheese. **Yield:** 12-14 servings (3-1/4 quarts).

Stuffed Sweet Pepper Soup

Joseph Kendra, Coraopolis, Pennsylvania

Tomatoes, peppers, garlic and onions are the mainstays of my garden. This soup puts my bounty to good use. It tastes just like classic stuffed peppers. Being the oldest of seven children, I acquired a knack for cooking early on in age from my mom.

>   1 pound ground beef
>   2 quarts water
>   1 quart tomato juice
>   3 medium sweet red *or* green peppers, diced
> 1-1/2 cups chili sauce
>   1 cup uncooked long grain rice
>   2 celery ribs, diced
>   1 large onion, diced
>   2 teaspoons browning sauce, optional
>   3 chicken bouillon cubes
>   2 garlic cloves, minced
> 1/2 teaspoon salt

In a large kettle or Dutch oven over medium heat, cook beef until no longer pink; drain. Add the remaining ingredients; bring to a boil. Reduce heat; simmer, uncovered, for 1 hour or until the rice is tender. **Yield:** 16 servings (4 quarts).

Santa Fe Chicken Chili

(Pictured below)

Sonia Gallant, St. Thomas, Ontario

Stir up a big pot of this chili on a Sunday, and you'll be all set for a couple of weekday meals later that week.

Chili powder, cumin and cayenne pepper add just the right amount of zip to this chili, which features chicken instead of the usual ground beef.

>   2 pounds boneless skinless chicken breasts, cut into 1/2-inch cubes
>   4 medium sweet red peppers, diced
>   4 garlic cloves, minced
>   2 large onions, chopped
> 1/4 cup olive *or* vegetable oil
>   3 tablespoons chili powder
>   2 teaspoons ground cumin
> 1/4 teaspoon cayenne pepper
>   1 can (28 ounces) diced tomatoes, undrained
>   2 cans (14-1/2 ounces *each*) chicken broth
>   2 cans (15-1/2 ounces *each*) kidney beans, rinsed and drained
>   1 jar (12 ounces) salsa
>   1 package (10 ounces) frozen corn
> 1/2 teaspoon salt
> 1/2 teaspoon pepper

In a 5-qt. kettle or Dutch oven over medium heat, saute chicken, peppers, garlic and onions in oil until the chicken is no longer pink and vegetables are tender, about 5-7 minutes.

Add chili powder, cumin and cayenne pepper; cook and stir for 1 minute. Add the tomatoes and broth; bring to a boil. Reduce heat; simmer, uncovered, for 15 minutes. Stir in remaining ingredients; bring to a boil. Reduce heat; cover and simmer for 10-15 minutes or until the chicken is tender. **Yield:** 14-16 servings (4 quarts).

Barbecued Pork Sandwiches

Karla Labby, Otsego, Michigan

When our office held a bridal shower for a co-worker, we presented the future bride with a collection of our favorite recipes. I included this one. I like serving this savory pork as an alternative to a typical ground beef barbecue.

>   2 boneless pork loin roasts (2-1/2 to 3 pounds *each*)
>   1 cup water
>   2 teaspoons salt
>   2 cups ketchup
>   2 cups diced celery
> 1/3 cup steak sauce
> 1/4 cup packed brown sugar
> 1/4 cup vinegar
>   2 teaspoons lemon juice
>   20 to 25 hamburger buns

Place roasts in an 8-qt. Dutch oven; add water and salt. Cover and cook on medium-low heat for 2-1/2 hours or until meat is tender. Remove roasts and shred with a fork; set aside.

Skim fat from cooking liquid and discard. Drain all but 1 cup cooking liquid. Add meat, ketchup, celery, steak sauce, brown sugar, vinegar and lemon juice. Cover and cook over medium-low heat for 1-1/2 hours. Serve on buns. **Yield:** 20-25 servings.

Savory Chicken Vegetable Strudel

(Pictured below)

Michele Barneson, Washburn, Wisconsin

If you're looking for a way to "sneak" vegetables into a dish, try this one that looks fancy without the fuss. Now that our two sons are grown, I make it for my husband and me. It is definitely a recipe for company as well, though.

- 2 cups diced cooked chicken
- 1/2 cup shredded carrots
- 1/2 cup finely chopped fresh broccoli
- 1/3 cup finely chopped sweet red pepper
- 1 cup (4 ounces) shredded sharp cheddar cheese
- 1/2 cup mayonnaise
- 2 garlic cloves, minced
- 1/2 teaspoon dill weed
- 1/4 teaspoon salt
- 1/4 teaspoon pepper
- 2 tubes (8 ounces *each*) refrigerated crescent rolls
- 1 egg white, beaten
- 2 tablespoons slivered almonds

In a bowl, combine the first 10 ingredients; mix well. Unroll crescent dough and place in a greased 15-in. x 10-in. x 1-in. baking pan; press seams and perforations together, forming a 15-in. x 12-in. rectangle (dough will hang over edges of pan). Spread filling lengthwise down the center of dough.

On each long side, cut 1-1/2-in.-wide strips 3-1/2 in. into center. Starting at one end, alternate strips, twisting twice and laying at an angle across filling. Seal ends. Brush dough with egg white; sprinkle with almonds. Bake at 375° for 30-35 minutes or until golden brown. Cut into slices; serve warm. **Yield:** 12 servings.

Shredded Barbecued Beef

(Pictured above)

Jesse and Anne Foust, Bluefield, West Virginia

Once family and friends have dug into this tender and tangy barbecued beef, you'll be making it again and again. It takes a little time to prepare, but it's well worth the effort for a picnic or dinner anytime.

- 1 boneless beef chuck roast (about 4 pounds)
- 3 tablespoons vegetable oil, *divided*
- 2 large onions, chopped
- 1 cup ketchup
- 1 cup beef broth
- 2/3 cup chili sauce
- 1/4 cup cider vinegar
- 1/4 cup packed brown sugar
- 3 tablespoons Worcestershire sauce
- 2 tablespoons prepared mustard
- 2 tablespoons molasses
- 2 tablespoons lemon juice
- 1 teaspoon salt
- 1/4 teaspoon cayenne pepper
- 1/8 teaspoon pepper
- 1 tablespoon liquid smoke, optional
- 12 to 16 kaiser rolls *or* hamburger buns

In a Dutch oven, brown roast on all sides in 1 tablespoon oil. Meanwhile, in a large saucepan, saute onions in remaining oil until tender. Add remaining ingredients except rolls; bring to a boil. Reduce heat; simmer, uncovered, for 15 minutes, stirring occasionally.

Pour over roast. Cover and bake at 325° for 2 hours; turn the roast and bake for 2 more hours or until meat is very tender. Remove roast; shred with a fork and return to sauce. Serve on rolls. **Yield:** 12-16 servings.

1/2 cup chopped onion
1 can (12 ounces) tomato paste
1 can (15 ounces) tomato sauce
1 cup water
1 tablespoon sugar
4 garlic cloves, minced
2 teaspoons dried basil
1 teaspoon dried oregano
1 teaspoon salt
20 sandwich buns
Shredded mozzarella cheese, optional

In a large Dutch oven, brown sausages a few at a time; discard all but 2 tablespoons drippings. Saute peppers and onion in drippings until crisp-tender; drain. Return sausages to pan along with tomato paste, tomato sauce, water, sugar, garlic, basil, oregano and salt; bring to a boil. Reduce heat; cover and simmer for 30 minutes. Serve on buns. Top with cheese if desired. **Yield:** 20 servings.

Sandwich for a Crowd

(Pictured above)

Helen Hougland, Spring Hill, Kansas

My husband and I live on a 21-acre horse ranch and are pleased to invite friends to enjoy it with us. When entertaining, I rely on no-fuss make-ahead entrees like this satisfying sandwich.

2 unsliced loaves (1 pound *each*) Italian bread
1 package (8 ounces) cream cheese, softened
1 cup (4 ounces) shredded cheddar cheese
3/4 cup sliced green onions
1/4 cup mayonnaise
1 tablespoon Worcestershire sauce
1 pound thinly sliced fully cooked ham
1 pound thinly sliced roast beef
12 to 14 thin slices dill pickle

Cut the bread in half lengthwise. Hollow out top and bottom of loaves, leaving a 1/2-in. shell (discard removed bread or save for another use).

Combine cheeses, onions, mayonnaise and Worcestershire sauce; spread over cut sides of bread. Layer ham and roast beef on bottom and top halves; place pickles on bottom halves. Gently press halves together. Wrap in plastic wrap and refrigerate for at least 2 hours. Cut into 1-1/2-in. slices. **Yield:** 12-14 servings.

Barbecued Hot Dogs

Joyce Koehler, Watertown, Wisconsin

I grew up in a family of eight kids, and we never complained if Mom made these terrific hot dogs often for birthday parties and other family gatherings. You'll find that kids and grown-ups devour these...good thing they're easy to make.

3/4 cup chopped onion
3 tablespoons butter *or* margarine
1-1/2 cups chopped celery
1-1/2 cups ketchup
3/4 cup water
1/3 cup lemon juice
3 tablespoons brown sugar
3 tablespoons vinegar
1 tablespoon Worcestershire sauce
1 tablespoon yellow mustard
2 packages (1 pound *each*) hot dogs
20 hot dog buns, split

In a saucepan over medium heat, saute onion in butter until tender. Add celery, ketchup, water, lemon juice, sugar, vinegar, Worcestershire sauce and mustard; bring to a boil. Reduce heat; cover and simmer for 30 minutes.

Cut three 1/4-in.-deep slits on each side of hot dogs; place in a 2-1/2-qt. baking dish. Pour sauce over hot dogs. Cover and bake at 350° for 40-45 minutes or until heated through. Serve on buns. **Yield:** 20 servings.

Italian Sausage Sandwiches

Mike Yaeger, Brookings, South Dakota

When my wife and I have friends over, we love to serve these sandwiches. This is a convenient recipe, since it can be prepared the day before and reheated.

20 Italian sausages
4 large green peppers, thinly sliced

Sandwich Savvy

ANYTIME you make sandwiches in advance, be sure to wrap them airtight and refrigerate. They'll keep for at least a day this way.

Glazed Corned Beef Sandwiches

(Pictured below)

Rita Reifenstein, Evans City, Pennsylvania

Fans of good food will cheer when you bring out these full-flavored, hearty sandwiches! Made of tender corned beef and a special sweet and spicy seasoning, they're always a hit. I serve them year-round, but they're especially popular on St. Patrick's Day.

```
1 corned beef brisket (3 to 4 pounds)
12 peppercorns
4 bay leaves
3 garlic cloves, minced
2 cinnamon sticks (3 inches), broken
1 tablespoon crushed red pepper flakes
Sandwich buns
GLAZE:
1/2 cup packed brown sugar
1/2 teaspoon ground cloves
1/2 teaspoon ground ginger
1/2 teaspoon ground mustard
1/4 teaspoon celery salt
1/4 teaspoon caraway seed
```

Place corned beef with seasoning packet in a Dutch oven; cover with water. Add seasonings and bring to a boil. Reduce heat; cover and simmer for 4 to 4-1/2 hours or until meat is tender. Drain, discarding juices; blot brisket dry.

In a small bowl, combine all of the glaze ingredients. Rub onto top of warm meat. Grill or broil for 5-10 minutes on each side until glazed. Slice meat and serve warm or chilled on buns. **Yield:** 12-16 servings.

Potluck Pockets

(Pictured above)

Debbie Jones, California, Maryland

My husband taught me how to make these fun tasty sandwiches. They take little time to prepare, and we enjoy them all through the year.

```
1 pound ground beef
1/2 cup chopped onion
1/2 cup chopped green pepper
2 tablespoons Worcestershire sauce
2 tablespoons soy sauce
2 teaspoons garlic powder
1 teaspoon ground cumin
1/2 teaspoon Italian seasoning
6 pita breads, halved
2 medium tomatoes, diced
3 cups shredded lettuce
SAUCE:
1/2 cup soy sauce
1/4 cup vinegar
2 tablespoons Worcestershire sauce
1/2 teaspoon onion powder
1/2 teaspoon garlic powder
1/2 teaspoon Italian seasoning
Dash pepper
```

In a skillet, cook beef, onion and green pepper until meat is no longer pink and vegetables are tender; drain. Add Worcestershire sauce, soy sauce, garlic powder, cumin and Italian seasoning; mix well. Simmer for 5-10 minutes. In a small saucepan, bring all the sauce ingredients to a boil. Reduce heat and simmer for 5-10 minutes. Spoon meat mixture into pita halves; top with sauce, tomatoes and lettuce. **Yield:** 12 servings.

Sandwich for 12

(Pictured above)

Melissa Collier, Wichita Falls, Texas

This super sandwich makes a fun supper, and it's also a great way of feeding your bunch lunch. A co-worker at the post office, who is one of the best cooks I know, shared the recipe with me.

      1/2 cup old-fashioned oats
      1/2 cup boiling water
        2 tablespoons butter *or* margarine
        1 package (16 ounces) hot roll mix
      3/4 cup warm water (110° to 115°)
        2 eggs, beaten
        1 tablespoon dried minced onion
    TOPPING:
        1 egg
        1 teaspoon garlic salt
        1 tablespoon dried minced onion
        1 tablespoon sesame seeds
    FILLING:
      1/2 cup mayonnaise
        4 teaspoons prepared mustard
      1/2 teaspoon prepared horseradish
    Lettuce leaves
        8 ounces thinly sliced fully cooked ham
        8 ounces thinly sliced cooked turkey
        1 medium green pepper, thinly sliced
        1 medium onion, thinly sliced
        6 ounces thinly sliced Swiss cheese
        2 large tomatoes, thinly sliced

In a large bowl, combine oats, boiling water and butter; let stand for 5 minutes. Meanwhile, dissolve yeast from hot roll mix in warm water. Add to the oat mixture with eggs and onion. Add flour mixture from hot roll mix; stir well (do not knead). Spread dough into a 10-in. circle on a well-greased pizza pan. Cover with plastic wrap

coated with nonstick cooking spray; let rise in a warm place until doubled, about 45 minutes.

Beat egg and garlic salt; brush gently over dough. Sprinkle with onion and sesame seeds. Bake at 350° for 25-30 minutes or until golden brown. Remove from pan; cool on a wire rack. Split lengthwise. Combine mayonnaise, mustard and horseradish; spread over cut sides of loaf. Layer with remaining filling ingredients. Cut into wedges. **Yield:** 12 servings.

All-American Barbecue Sandwiches

(Pictured below)

Sue Gronholz, Columbus, Wisconsin

I came up with this delicious recipe on my own. It's my husband's favorite and is a big hit with family and friends who enjoyed it at our Fourth of July picnic.

    4-1/2 pounds ground beef
    1-1/2 cups chopped onion
    2-1/4 cups ketchup
        3 tablespoons prepared mustard
        3 tablespoons Worcestershire sauce
        2 tablespoons vinegar
        2 tablespoons sugar
        1 tablespoon salt
        1 tablespoon pepper
       18 hamburger buns, split

In a Dutch oven, cook beef and onion until meat is no longer pink and onion is tender; drain. Combine ketchup, mustard, Worcestershire, vinegar, sugar, salt and pepper; stir into beef mixture. Heat through. Serve on buns. **Yield:** 18 servings.

Savory Pork Turnovers

(Pictured at right)

Ruby Carves, Litchfield, Maine

Apples, potatoes, ground pork and seasonings tucked inside flaky golden pastry never fail to win praise from my family at home and friends at church functions. The assembly requires a bit of effort, but these impressive little turnovers are worth it.

    6 cups all-purpose flour
    2 teaspoons sugar
1-1/2 teaspoons salt
    1 cup shortening
    1 cup cold butter *or* margarine
  12 to 18 tablespoons cold water
FILLING:
    2 pounds ground pork
    3 tablespoons butter *or* margarine
  1/2 cup chopped onion
    2 cups cooked cubed peeled potatoes
    2 cups diced peeled tart apples
    3 tablespoons all-purpose flour
    1 tablespoon brown sugar
1-1/2 teaspoons rubbed sage
    1 teaspoon pepper
  1/2 teaspoon salt
    2 egg yolks
    2 tablespoons water

In a bowl, combine flour, sugar and salt; cut in the short ening and butter until crumbly. Add water, 1 tablespoon at a time, tossing lightly with a fork until dough forms a ball. Cover and chill for at least 1 hour. In a Dutch oven over medium heat, brown pork until no longer pink; drain. Add butter and onion; saute until onion is tender. Add potatoes, apples, flour, sugar, sage, pepper and salt; cook and stir for 2 minutes. Cool.

Meanwhile, on a heavily floured surface, roll pastry to 1/8-in. thickness; cut into 3-1/2-in. circles. Place 1-2 tablespoons filling on each circle. Moisten edges with water; fold dough in half. Seal edges with fingers or a fork. Place on ungreased baking sheets. Beat egg yolks and water; brush over turnovers. Bake at 375° for 20-25 minutes or until golden brown. Serve warm. **Yield:** about 4 dozen.

Three-Meat Stromboli

Lorelei Hull, Luling, Louisiana

I made this hearty sandwich for a golf outing my husband attended and received many compliments on it. Several men asked for the recipe.

    2 loaves (1 pound *each*) frozen bread dough,
      thawed
    2 tablespoons Dijon mustard
  1/2 cup grated Parmesan cheese, *divided*
    4 ounces pastrami, finely chopped
    4 ounces pepperoni, finely chopped
    4 ounces salami, finely chopped
    1 cup (4 ounces) shredded Swiss cheese
    1 egg, beaten

Roll each loaf of bread into a 12-in. x 7-in. rectangle. Spread mustard to within 1 in. of edges. Sprinkle each with 2 tablespoons of Parmesan cheese. Combine pastrami, pepperoni, salami and Swiss cheese; sprinkle over top of the dough. Top with the remaining Parmesan cheese.

Brush edges of dough with egg. Roll up, jelly-roll style, beginning with a long side. Seal edge and ends. Place seam side down on a greased baking sheet; cut three slits in the top of each loaf. Bake at 350° for 35-40 minutes. Slice; serve warm. **Yield:** 2 loaves (12-16 servings each).

Shredded Pork Sandwiches

Judi Jones, Wadsworth, Ohio

I received this recipe from my sister Linda. Her recipes are always delicious because she's an excellent cook.

    1 boneless pork shoulder roast (3 to 4 pounds)
1-1/4 cups ketchup
  1/2 cup water
  1/2 cup chopped celery
  1/4 cup chopped onion
  1/4 cup lemon juice
    3 tablespoons vinegar
    2 tablespoons Worcestershire sauce
    2 tablespoons brown sugar
1-1/2 teaspoons ground mustard
    1 teaspoon salt
  1/2 teaspoon pepper
  12 to 14 hamburger buns, split

Place roast in a Dutch oven or large kettle. In a bowl, combine the ketchup, water, celery, onion, lemon juice, vinegar, Worcestershire sauce, brown sugar, mustard, salt and pepper; pour over roast. Cover and cook over medium-low heat for 4-6 hours or until meat is tender and pulls apart easily. Shred meat with two forks. Serve on buns. **Yield:** 12-14 servings.

Main Dishes

Baked Spaghetti (p. 63)

Chapter 5

1 can (12 ounces) evaporated milk
1 cup milk
1/2 cup chicken broth
1/2 cup mayonnaise*
2 tablespoons lemon juice
2 teaspoons grated onion
2 teaspoons prepared mustard
2 teaspoons minced fresh parsley
1/4 teaspoon dried rosemary, crushed
1/2 cup shredded cheddar cheese
3 cups cubed fully cooked ham

Cook spaghetti according to package directions; rinse with cold water and drain. In a large saucepan, bring 2 cups of water to a boil. Add asparagus. Cover and cook for 3-5 minutes or until crisp-tender; drain. In a bowl, toss spaghetti with eggs and 1/4 cup Parmesan cheese. Spread into two greased 2-qt. baking dishes.

In a large saucepan, melt butter. Stir in flour until smooth. Gradually add the evaporated milk, milk and broth. Bring to a boil; cook and stir for 1-2 minutes or until thickened. Remove from the heat. Whisk in the mayonnaise, lemon juice, onion, mustard, parsley and rosemary. Stir in cheddar cheese and remaining Parmesan until blended.

Sprinkle ham and asparagus over spaghetti crusts. Pour cheese sauce over top. Cover and bake at 350° for 40 minutes. Uncover; bake 5-10 minutes longer or until edges are bubbly. **Yield:** 2 casseroles (10 servings each).

*Editor's Note: Reduced-fat or fat-free mayonnaise may not be substituted for regular mayonnaise.

No-Fuss Chicken

(Pictured above)

Marilyn Dick, Centralia, Missouri

This recipe could hardly be simpler to prepare. The chicken gets a tangy taste, and no one will know you used convenient ingredients like a bottle of salad dressing and onion soup mix...unless you tell them.

1 bottle (16 ounces) Russian *or* Catalina salad dressing
2/3 cup apricot preserves
2 envelopes dry onion soup mix
16 boneless skinless chicken breast halves
Hot cooked rice

In a bowl, combine dressing, preserves and soup mix. Place chicken in two ungreased 11-in. x 7-in. x 2-in. baking pans; top with dressing mixture. Cover and bake at 350° for 20 minutes; baste. Bake, uncovered, 20 minutes longer or until chicken juices run clear. Serve over rice. **Yield:** 16 servings.

Ham and Asparagus Casserole

Kea Fisher, Bridger, Montana

We eat this tasty casserole often, so I like to change the ingredients now and then. I'll double the amount of rosemary, substitute green beans or broccoli for the asparagus or use chicken instead of ham.

1 package (16 ounces) spaghetti, broken into thirds
2 pounds fresh asparagus, trimmed and cut into 1-1/2 inch pieces
2 eggs, lightly beaten
1/2 cup grated Parmesan cheese, *divided*
1/4 cup butter *or* margarine
1/4 cup all-purpose flour

Company Casserole

Marcia McCutchan, Hamilton, Ohio

I concocted this recipe one day while trying to straighten up my canned goods cupboard. Friends and relatives have told me how much they like it.

8 ounces process cheese (Velveeta), cubed
1/4 cup milk
2 cans (14-1/2 ounces *each*) diced tomatoes, undrained
3/4 cup mayonnaise *or* salad dressing*
1 tablespoon Worcestershire sauce
4 cups cubed fully cooked ham
4 cups cooked elbow macaroni
1 package (10 ounces) frozen chopped broccoli, thawed and drained
1 package (10 ounces) frozen peas, thawed
1 small green pepper, chopped
1 small onion, chopped
1/2 cup crushed stuffing mix
1 can (2.8 ounces) french-fried onions, chopped, optional
1 cup soft bread crumbs
1/4 cup butter *or* margarine, melted

In a large saucepan, cook and stir cheese and milk over low heat until cheese is melted. Stir in tomatoes until blended. Remove from the heat; stir in the mayonnaise and Worcestershire sauce until blended. Stir in the ham, macaroni, broccoli, peas, green pepper, onion, stuffing mix and onions if desired.

Transfer to two greased 2-1/2-qt. baking dishes. Toss bread crumbs and butter; sprinkle over the top. Bake, uncovered, at 350° for 35-40 minutes or until bubbly. **Yield:** 2 casseroles (8-10 servings each).

*Editor's Note: Reduced-fat or fat-free mayonnaise or salad dressing may not be substituted for regular mayonnaise or salad dressing.

Holiday Ham with Pineapple

(Pictured below)

Sue Jackson-Tucker, Sunset, Utah

My husband and I have lots of family living in our area, so any gathering is bound to be big. This ham satisfies everyone and is often requested. One of my brothers-in-law will eat six slices of this ham before helping himself to anything else. We never have leftovers.

  1 whole bone-in fully cooked ham (12 to 14 pounds), spiral-cut* *or* thinly sliced
  2 cans (6 ounces *each*) pineapple juice
  1 can (20 ounces) crushed pineapple, undrained
  2 cups packed brown sugar
  20 to 30 whole cloves
  1/4 cup golden raisins

Place the ham in a roasting pan. Slowly pour pineapple juice over the ham so it runs between the slices. Spoon pineapple over the ham. Sprinkle with brown sugar and cloves. Add raisins to the pan juices. Cover and refrigerate overnight. Discard cloves. Cover and bake ham at 325° for 1-1/2 to 2 hours or until a meat thermometer reads 140°, basting every 20 minutes. **Yield:** 24-28 servings.

*Editor's Note: If spiral-cut ham is not available, ask your butcher to cut a fully cooked ham into 1/8-in.-thick slices and tie it securely.

Dinner in a Dish

(Pictured above)

Betty Sitzman, Wray, Colorado

I haven't found anyone yet who can resist this saucy beef casserole topped with mashed potatoes. The peas and tomatoes add color and make a helping or two a complete meal.

  2 pounds ground beef
  1 medium onion, chopped
  2 cans (14-1/2 ounces *each*) diced tomatoes, undrained
  3 cups frozen peas
  2/3 cup ketchup
  1/4 cup chopped fresh parsley
  2 tablespoons all-purpose flour
  2 teaspoons beef bouillon granules
  2 teaspoons dried marjoram
  1 teaspoon salt
  1/2 teaspoon pepper
  6 cups hot mashed potatoes (prepared with milk and butter)
  2 eggs

In a saucepan over medium heat, cook the beef and onion until meat is no longer pink; drain. Add the next nine ingredients; mix well. Bring to a boil; cook and stir for 2 minutes. Pour into an ungreased shallow 3-qt. baking dish. Combine potatoes and eggs; mix well. Drop by 1/2 cupfuls onto beef mixture. Bake, uncovered, at 350° for 35-40 minutes or until bubbly and potatoes are lightly browned. **Yield:** 12 servings.

Pizza Meatballs

(Pictured below)

Kim Kanatzar, Blue Springs, Missouri

With mozzarella cheese inside, these tender meatballs taste almost like pizza. They're a hit with all ages at all sorts of gatherings.

    2 cups seasoned bread crumbs
    1 cup milk
    1/4 cup dried minced onion
    2 teaspoons garlic salt
    1/4 teaspoon pepper
    2 pounds ground beef
    1 block (8 ounces) mozzarella cheese
    1/3 cup all-purpose flour
    1/4 cup vegetable oil
    2 jars (28 ounces *each*) pizza sauce

In a bowl, combine the first five ingredients; crumble beef over mixture and mix well. Shape into 48 meatballs. Cut mozzarella into 48 cubes, 1/2 in. each; push a cube into the center of each meatball, covering the cheese completely with meat. Roll lightly in flour.

In a large skillet, cook meatballs in oil until browned; drain. Add pizza sauce; bring to a boil. Reduce heat; cover and simmer for 25-30 minutes or until meatballs are no longer pink. **Yield:** 4 dozen.

Classic Lasagna

Suzanne Barker, Bellingham, Washington

A definite crowd-pleaser, this classic lasagna is thick, rich and meaty with lots of cheese—just the way I like it. Even though my parents were Hungarian, I have a weakness for savory Italian foods like this.

    1/2 pound bulk Italian sausage
    1/2 pound ground beef
    1-1/2 cups diced onion
    1 cup diced carrot
    3 garlic cloves, minced
    1/4 teaspoon crushed red pepper flakes

    2 cans (28 ounces *each*) whole tomatoes,
      undrained
    2 tablespoons tomato paste
    1 teaspoon *each* sugar, dried oregano and basil
    1 teaspoon pepper, *divided*
    1 teaspoon salt
    2 cartons (15 ounces *each*) ricotta cheese
    3/4 cup grated Parmesan cheese, *divided*
    1 egg
    1/3 cup minced fresh parsley
    1 package (12 ounces) lasagna noodles, cooked,
      rinsed and drained
    2 cups (8 ounces) shredded mozzarella cheese

In a large saucepan over medium heat, cook sausage, beef, onion, carrot, garlic and pepper flakes until meat is no longer pink and vegetables are tender; drain. Add tomatoes, tomato paste, sugar, oregano, basil, 1/2 teaspoon pepper and salt; bring to a boil. Reduce heat; simmer, uncovered, for 45 minutes or until thick, stirring occasionally.

Combine ricotta, 1/2 cup Parmesan cheese, egg, parsley and remaining pepper. In a greased 13-in. x 9-in. x 2-in. baking dish, layer a fourth of the noodles, a third of the ricotta mixture, a fourth of the meat sauce and 1/2 cup mozzarella cheese. Repeat layers twice. Top with the remaining noodles, sauce and Parmesan. Cover and bake at 400° for 45 minutes. Sprinkle with remaining mozzarella; bake, uncovered, 10 minutes more. Let stand 15 minutes before serving. **Yield:** 12 servings.

Savory Pot Roast

Lee Leuschner, Calgary, Alberta

My husband and I used to raise cattle, so I prepared a lot of beef. This old-fashioned pot roast is the best— smooth gravy is a tempting topper for the tender, flavorful meat. I like to serve it with crisp potato pancakes.

    1 rolled boneless chuck roast* (6 pounds)
    2 tablespoons vegetable oil
    1 large onion, coarsely chopped
    2 medium carrots, coarsely chopped
    1 celery rib, coarsely chopped
    2 cups water
    1 can (14-1/2 ounces) beef broth
    2 bay leaves
GRAVY:
    1/4 cup butter *or* margarine
    1/4 cup all-purpose flour
    1 teaspoon lemon juice
    4 to 5 drops hot pepper sauce

In a large skillet over medium-high heat, brown roast on all sides in oil. Transfer to a large roasting pan; add onion, carrots and celery. In a saucepan, bring water, broth and bay leaves to a boil. Pour over roast and vegetables. Cover and bake at 350° for 2-1/2 to 3 hours or until meat is tender, turning once. Remove roast to a serving platter and keep warm.

For gravy, strain pan juices, reserving 2 cups. Discard

vegetables are tender; drain. Add tomato sauce and paste, water and seasonings; bring to a boil. Reduce heat; cover and simmer for 15 minutes. Add corn and olives; cover and simmer for 5 minutes. Stir in noodles. Pour into two greased 13-in. x 9-in. x 2-in. baking dishes. Top with cheese. Cover and bake at 350° for 25-30 minutes or until heated through. **Yield:** 16-20 servings.

Potluck Spareribs

(Pictured below)

Sheri Kirkman, Lancaster, New York

These ribs are perfect for a potluck...I never have leftovers. I've been making family meals since I was 13. Now I love cooking for my husband and children.

 6 pounds pork spareribs
1-1/2 cups ketchup
 3/4 cup packed brown sugar
 1/2 cup vinegar
 1/2 cup honey
 1/3 cup soy sauce
1-1/2 teaspoons ground ginger
 1 teaspoon salt
 3/4 teaspoon ground mustard
 1/2 teaspoon garlic powder
 1/4 teaspoon pepper

Cut ribs into serving-size pieces; place with the meaty side up on racks in two greased 13-in. x 9-in. x 2-in. baking pans. Cover tightly with foil. Bake at 350° for 1-1/4 hours or until meat is tender.

Drain; remove racks and return ribs to pans. Combine remaining ingredients; pour over ribs. Return to the oven, uncovered, for 35 minutes or until sauce coats ribs, basting occasionally. Ribs can also be grilled over medium-hot heat for the last 35 minutes instead of baking. **Yield:** 12 servings.

vegetables and bay leaves. In a saucepan over medium heat, melt butter. Stir in flour until smooth. Gradually stir in pan juices; bring to a boil. Cook and stir for 2 minutes. Add lemon juice and hot pepper sauce; mix well. Serve with the roast. **Yield:** 14-16 servings.

*Editor's Note: Ask your butcher to tie two 3-pound chuck roasts together to form a rolled chuck roast.

Italian Casserole

(Pictured above)

Rita Goshaw, South Milwaukee, Wisconsin

I come from a huge family, and it seems there is always a potluck occasion. Come spring, graduation parties are the perfect place for me to bring this hearty, crowd-pleasing Italian main dish. It's both easy to make and serve.

1-1/2 pounds bulk Italian sausage
1-1/2 pounds ground beef
 1 cup chopped onion
 1 cup chopped green pepper
 2 cans (15 ounces *each*) tomato sauce
 2 cans (6 ounces *each*) tomato paste
 1/2 cup water
 1 teaspoon dried basil
 1 teaspoon dried oregano
 1 teaspoon salt
 1 teaspoon pepper
 1/8 teaspoon garlic powder
 2 cans (8-3/4 ounces *each*) whole kernel corn, drained
 2 cans (2-1/4 ounces *each*) sliced ripe olives, drained
 1 package (16 ounces) wide noodles, cooked and drained
 8 ounces cheddar cheese, cut into strips

In a Dutch oven over medium heat, cook sausage, beef, onion and green pepper until meat is browned and

1 can (8 ounces) sliced mushrooms, drained
1 jar (2 ounces) chopped pimientos, drained
1/2 teaspoon dried basil
1 package (8 ounces) noodles, cooked and drained
3 cups diced cooked chicken
2 cups ricotta *or* cottage cheese
2 cups (8 ounces) shredded cheddar cheese
1/2 cup grated Parmesan cheese
1/4 cup buttered bread crumbs

In a skillet, saute onion and green pepper in butter until tender. Remove from the heat. Stir in the soup, mushrooms, pimientos and basil; set aside. In a large bowl, combine noodles, chicken and cheeses; add mushroom sauce and mix well. Transfer to a greased 13-in. x 9-in. x 2-in. baking dish. Bake, uncovered, at 350° for 40-45 minutes or until bubbly. Sprinkle with crumbs. Bake 15 minutes longer. **Yield:** 12-15 servings.

Tangy Meatballs

Jane Barta, St. Thomas, North Dakota

These savory meatballs are a family favorite and a big hit wherever they go. In their delicious barbecue sauce, they're a perfect dish to pass.

2 eggs
2 cups quick-cooking *or* rolled oats
1 can (12 ounces) evaporated milk
1 cup chopped onion
2 teaspoons salt
1/2 teaspoon pepper
1/2 teaspoon garlic powder
3 pounds lean ground beef
SAUCE:
2 cups ketchup
1-1/2 cups packed brown sugar
1/2 cup chopped onion
1 to 2 teaspoons liquid smoke, optional
1/2 teaspoon garlic powder

In a large bowl, beat eggs. Add oats, milk, onion, salt, pepper and garlic powder. Crumble beef over mixture and mix well. Shape into 1-1/2-in. balls. Place in two 13-in. x 9-in. x 2-in. baking pans. Bake, uncovered, at 375° for 30 minutes. Remove from the oven and drain. Place all of the meatballs in one of the pans.

In a saucepan, bring all of the sauce ingredients to a boil. Pour over meatballs. Return to the oven and bake, uncovered, for 20 minutes or until meatballs are no longer pink. **Yield:** 4 dozen.

Stuffed Pasta Shells

(Pictured above and on front cover)

Jena Coffey, St. Louis, Missouri

These savory shells never fail to make a big impression, even though the recipe is very easy. One or two of these shells makes a great individual serving at a potluck, so a single batch goes a long way.

4 cups (16 ounces) shredded mozzarella cheese
1 carton (15 ounces) ricotta cheese
1 package (10 ounces) frozen chopped spinach, thawed and drained
1 package (12 ounces) jumbo pasta shells, cooked and drained
1 jar (28 ounces) spaghetti sauce

Combine cheeses and spinach; stuff into shells. Arrange in a greased 13-in. x 9-in. x 2-in. baking dish. Pour spaghetti sauce over the shells. Cover and bake at 350° for 30 minutes or until heated through. **Yield:** 12-14 servings.

Three-Cheese Chicken Bake

Vicky Raatz, Waterloo, Wisconsin

This is a hearty, comforting casserole that's always a crowd-pleaser. The combination of flavors and interesting colors ensures I come home with an empty dish

1/2 cup chopped onion
1/2 cup chopped green pepper
3 tablespoons butter *or* margarine
1 can (10-3/4 ounces) condensed cream of chicken soup, undiluted

Pineapple Pepper Chicken

(Pictured at right)

Phyllis Minter, Wakefield, Kansas

I came up with this recipe years ago by combining a couple of family favorites. Easy and versatile, it's great for potlucks. I can make the sauce ahead and use all wings or leg quarters when they're on sale. This is a welcome entree at senior citizen fellowship dinners.

4 cups unsweetened pineapple juice
2-1/2 cups sugar
2 cups vinegar
1-1/2 cups water
1 cup packed brown sugar
2/3 cup cornstarch
1/2 cup ketchup
6 tablespoons soy sauce
2 teaspoons chicken bouillon granules
3/4 teaspoon ground ginger
3 tablespoons vegetable oil
2 broiler/fryer chickens (3 to 3-1/2 pounds *each*), cut up
1 can (8 ounces) pineapple chunks, drained
1 medium green pepper, julienned

In a saucepan, combine the first 10 ingredients; stir until smooth. Bring to a boil; cook and stir for 2 minutes or until thickened. Set aside. Heat oil in a large skillet over medium-high heat. Add the chicken; brown on all sides. Place in two greased 13-in. x 9-in. x 2-in. baking dishes. Pour reserved sauce over chicken.

Bake, uncovered, at 350° for 45 minutes. Add pineapple and green pepper. Bake 15 minutes longer or until heated through. **Yield:** 12 servings.

Four-Cheese Spinach Lasagna

(Pictured above right)

Kimberly Kneisly, Englewood, Ohio

This rich cheesy lasagna has become one of my specialties. It's packed with fresh-tasting vegetables like spinach, carrots, red pepper and broccoli. I'm never afraid to serve the colorful casserole to guests, since it's always a huge success.

2 cups chopped fresh broccoli
1-1/2 cups julienned carrots
1 cup sliced green onions
1/2 cup chopped sweet red pepper
3 garlic cloves, minced
2 teaspoons vegetable oil
1/2 cup all-purpose flour
3 cups milk
1/2 cup grated Parmesan cheese, *divided*
1/2 teaspoon salt
1/4 teaspoon pepper
1 package (10 ounces) frozen chopped spinach, thawed and well drained
1-1/2 cups small-curd cottage cheese
1 cup (4 ounces) shredded mozzarella cheese
1/2 cup shredded Swiss cheese
12 lasagna noodles, cooked and drained

In a skillet, saute the vegetables and garlic in oil until crisp-tender. Remove from the heat; set aside. In a heavy saucepan, whisk flour and milk until smooth. Bring to a boil; cook and stir for 2 minutes. Reduce heat; add 1/4 cup Parmesan cheese, salt and pepper. Cook 1 minute longer or until cheese is melted. Remove from the heat; stir in spinach. Set 1 cup aside.

In a bowl, combine cottage cheese, mozzarella and Swiss. Spread 1/2 cup spinach mixture in a greased 13-in. x 9-in. x 2-in. baking dish. Layer with four noodles, half of cheese mixture and vegetables and 3/4 cup spinach mixture. Repeat layers. Top with remaining noodles, reserved spinach mixture and remaining Parmesan cheese. Cover and bake at 375° for 35 minutes. Uncover; bake 15 minutes longer or until bubbly. Let stand 15 minutes before cutting. **Yield:** 12 servings.

a delicious side dish. It doesn't take long to make but tastes like it simmered all day.

- 3 pounds ground beef
- 2 medium onions, chopped
- 2 celery ribs, chopped
- 2 teaspoons beef bouillon granules
- 2/3 cup boiling water
- 2 cans (28 ounces *each*) baked beans with molasses
- 1-1/2 cups ketchup
- 1/4 cup prepared mustard
- 3 garlic cloves, minced
- 1-1/2 teaspoons salt
- 1/2 teaspoon pepper
- 1/2 pound sliced bacon, cooked and crumbled

In a Dutch oven over medium heat, cook beef, onions and celery until meat is no longer pink and vegetables are tender; drain. Dissolve bouillon in water; stir into beef mixture. Add the beans, ketchup, mustard, garlic, salt and pepper; mix well. Cover and bake at 375° for 60-70 minutes or until bubbly; stir. Top with bacon. **Yield:** 12 servings.

Kodiak Casserole

(Pictured above)

Kathy Crow, Cordova, Alaska

Because it packs a little kick and has an interesting and tasty mix of ingredients, this is the perfect potluck for fall—or any time. One of my husband's favorites, it's an Alaskan recipe I found in the early 1950s.

- 2 pounds ground beef
- 4 cups diced onions
- 2 garlic cloves, minced
- 3 medium green peppers, diced
- 4 cups diced celery
- 1 jar (5-3/4 ounces) stuffed green olives, undrained
- 1 can (4 ounces) mushroom stems and pieces, undrained
- 1 can (10-3/4 ounces) condensed tomato soup, undiluted
- 1 jar (8 ounces) picante sauce
- 1 bottle (18 ounces) barbecue sauce
- 2 tablespoons Worcestershire sauce
- 3 to 4 cups medium egg noodles, cooked and drained
- 1 cup (4 ounces) shredded cheddar cheese

In a Dutch oven, cook beef with onions and garlic until meat is no longer pink; drain. Add remaining ingredients except cheese; mix well. Cover and bake at 350° for 1 hour or until hot and bubbly. Sprinkle with the cheese just before serving. **Yield:** 16-20 servings.

Western-Style Beef 'n' Beans

Jolene Lopez, Wichita, Kansas

This hearty, crowd-pleasing dish is a comforting meal on a chilly night with bread and a salad. It also makes

Seafood Tortilla Lasagna

(Pictured below)

Sharon Sawicki, Carol Stream, Illinois

My husband and I enjoy lasagna, seafood and Mexican fare. One evening, I combined all three into this deliciously different entree. It certainly is a tempting, memorable change of pace from traditional Italian-style lasagnas.

- 1 jar (20 ounces) picante sauce
- 1-1/2 pounds uncooked medium shrimp, peeled and deveined
- 4 to 6 garlic cloves, minced
- 1/8 teaspoon cayenne pepper

1 tablespoon olive *or* vegetable oil
1/3 cup butter *or* margarine
1/3 cup all-purpose flour
1 can (14-1/2 ounces) chicken broth
1/2 cup whipping cream
15 corn tortillas (6 inches), warmed
1 package (16 ounces) imitation crabmeat, flaked
3 cups (12 ounces) shredded Colby/Monterey Jack cheese

Place the picante sauce in a blender or food processor; cover and process until smooth. Set aside. In a skillet, cook shrimp, garlic and cayenne in oil until shrimp turn pink, about 3 minutes; remove and set aside. In the same skillet, melt the butter. Stir in flour until smooth. Gradually add broth. Bring to a boil; cook and stir for 2 minutes or until thickened. Reduce heat. Stir in cream and picante sauce; heat through.

Spread 1/2 cup of sauce in a greased 13-in. x 9-in. x 2-in. baking dish. Layer with six tortillas, half of the shrimp, crab and white sauce and 1-1/4 cups cheese. Repeat layers. Tear or cut remaining tortillas; arrange over cheese. Sprinkle with remaining cheese. Bake, uncovered, at 375° for 30-35 minutes or until bubbly. Let stand 15 minutes before cutting. **Yield:** 12 servings.

Turkey Stir-Fry Supper

Mavis Diment, Marcus, Iowa

Tempting turkey is combined with rice, colorful vegetables and a mild sauce in this meal-in-one entree. I share it at many gatherings and get compliments in return.

☑ Uses less fat, sugar or salt. Includes Nutritional Analysis and Diabetic Exchanges.

2-1/4 pounds boneless skinless turkey breast
2 tablespoons vegetable oil
3/4 cup uncooked long grain rice
2 cans (14-1/2 ounces *each*) chicken broth, *divided*
5 tablespoons soy sauce
2 garlic cloves, minced
1/2 teaspoon ground ginger
1/4 teaspoon pepper
1 package (10 ounces) frozen broccoli spears, thawed
1 pound carrots, thinly sliced
3 bunches green onions, sliced
3 tablespoons cornstarch
1 can (14 ounces) bean sprouts, drained

Cut turkey into 2-in. strips. In a Dutch oven or wok, stir-fry turkey in batches in oil for 5-7 minutes or until juices run clear. Set turkey aside. Add rice, 3-1/2 cups broth, soy sauce, garlic, ginger and pepper to pan; bring to a boil. Reduce heat; cover and simmer for 15 minutes or until rice is tender.

Cut broccoli into 3-in. pieces. Add broccoli, carrots and onions to rice mixture; simmer for 3-5 minutes. Combine cornstarch and remaining broth; add to pan. Bring to a boil; cook and stir for 2 minutes. Stir in turkey and bean sprouts; heat through. **Yield:** 14 servings.

Nutritional Analysis: One 1-cup serving (prepared with reduced-sodium broth and reduced-sodium soy sauce) equals 233 calories, 345 mg sodium, 46 mg cholesterol, 19 gm carbohydrate, 22 gm protein, 8 gm fat. **Diabetic Exchanges:** 2 meat, 1 starch, 1 vegetable.

Orange-Glazed Pork Loin

(Pictured below)

Lynnette Miete, Alna, Maine

This is one of the best pork recipes I've ever tried. My family looks forward to this roast for dinner and guests always want the recipe. The flavorful rub and a glaze sparked with orange juice are also outstanding on pork chops.

1 teaspoon salt
1 garlic clove, minced
1/4 teaspoon dried thyme
1/4 teaspoon ground ginger
1/4 teaspoon pepper
1 rolled boneless pork loin roast (about 5 pounds)
GLAZE:
1/4 cup packed brown sugar
1 tablespoon cornstarch
1 cup orange juice
1/3 cup water
1 tablespoon Dijon mustard

Combine the salt, garlic, thyme, ginger and pepper; rub over entire roast. Place roast with fat side up on a rack in a shallow roasting pan. Bake, uncovered, at 350° for 2 hours.

Meanwhile, in a saucepan, combine brown sugar and cornstarch. Stir in the remaining glaze ingredients until smooth. Bring to a boil; cook and stir for 2 minutes. Brush some of the glaze over roast. Bake 1 hour longer or until a meat thermometer reads 160°, brushing occasionally with glaze. Let stand for 10 minutes before slicing; serve with remaining glaze. **Yield:** 12-16 servings.

advance and freeze them. Then she only needs to bake them before dinner.

advance and freeze them. Then she only needs to bake them before dinner.

> 2 eggs
> 1 cup evaporated milk
> 1-1/2 cups graham cracker crumbs (about 22 squares)
> 1-1/4 pounds ground fully cooked ham
> 1-1/4 pounds bulk pork sausage
> 1 can (10-3/4 ounces) condensed tomato soup, undiluted
> 1 cup plus 2 tablespoons packed brown sugar
> 1/3 cup vinegar
> 1 teaspoon ground mustard

In a bowl, combine eggs, milk and cracker crumbs; mix well. Add ham and sausage. Shape 1/2 cupfuls into individual loaves. Place in a greased 13-in. x 9-in. x 2-in. baking dish. Combine the soup, brown sugar, vinegar and mustard; mix well. Pour over loaves. Bake, uncovered, at 350° for 1 hour, basting after 30 minutes. **Yield:** 12-14 servings.

Baked Rice with Sausage

(Pictured above)

Naomi Flood, Emporia, Kansas

This recipe is perfect for potlucks or church suppers since it produces a big batch and has flavors with broad appeal.

> 2 pounds bulk Italian sausage
> 4 celery ribs, thinly sliced
> 1 large onion, chopped
> 1 large green pepper, chopped
> 4-1/2 cups water
> 3/4 cup dry chicken noodle soup mix (1-1/2 envelopes)
> 1 can (10-3/4 ounces) condensed cream of chicken soup, undiluted
> 1 cup uncooked long grain rice
> 1/4 cup dry bread crumbs
> 2 tablespoons butter *or* margarine, melted

In a large skillet, cook sausage, celery, onion and green pepper over medium heat until meat is no longer pink and vegetables are tender; drain. In a large saucepan, bring water to a boil; add dry soup mix. Reduce heat; simmer, uncovered, for 5 minutes or until the noodles are tender. Stir in canned soup, rice and sausage mixture; mix well.

Transfer to a greased 13-in. x 9-in. x 2-in. baking dish. Cover and bake at 350° for 40 minutes. Toss bread crumbs and butter; sprinkle over rice mixture. Bake, uncovered, for 10-15 minutes or until rice is tender. Let stand 10 minutes before serving. **Yield:** 12-14 servings.

Miniature Ham Loaves

Alyson Armstrong, Parkersburg, West Virginia

When there's a special dinner coming, Mom will usually prepare these scrumptious loaves several days in

Tangy Beef Brisket

Jacque Watkins, Green River, Wyoming

We like the sauce for my brisket over elk, moose and venison salami as well. And we also use it to spice hamburgers and hot dogs we sizzle on the grill.

> 1 large onion, diced
> 1/2 cup butter *or* margarine
> 1 bottle (28 ounces) ketchup
> 1-1/2 cups packed brown sugar
> 1/2 cup Worcestershire sauce
> 1/3 cup lemon juice
> 2 tablespoons chili powder
> 1-1/2 teaspoons hot pepper sauce
> 1 teaspoon prepared horseradish
> 1 teaspoon salt
> 1/2 teaspoon garlic powder
> 1 boneless beef brisket* (6 pounds)

In a saucepan, saute onion in butter until tender. Add the next nine ingredients; bring to a boil. Reduce heat; simmer, uncovered, for 30-40 minutes. Place brisket in a roasting pan. Add 3 cups of sauce. Cover and bake at 350° for 4 hours, basting occasionally. Skim fat. Remove brisket. Thinly slice beef; return to pan. Add remaining sauce. **Yield:** 12-14 servings (6 cups sauce).

*Editor's Note: This is a fresh beef brisket, not corned beef.

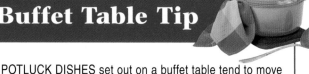

Buffet Table Tip

POTLUCK DISHES set out on a buffet table tend to move around when people scoop food from them. To prevent this from happening, just set a damp cloth napkin or dish towel underneath the dishes.

Main Dishes

Turkey Lattice Pie

(Pictured below)

Lorraine Naig, Emmetsburg, Iowa

With its pretty lattice crust, this cheesy baked dish is as eye-catching as it is delicious. It's easy to make, too, since it uses convenient crescent roll dough.

    3 tubes (8 ounces *each*) refrigerated crescent
      rolls
    4 cups cubed cooked turkey
1-1/2 cups (6 ounces) shredded cheddar *or* Swiss
      cheese
    1 package (10 ounces) frozen chopped broccoli,
      thawed and drained
    1 can (10-3/4 ounces) condensed cream of
      chicken soup, undiluted
1-1/3 cups milk
    2 tablespoons Dijon mustard
    1 tablespoon dried minced onion
  1/2 teaspoon salt
Dash pepper
    1 egg, lightly beaten

Unroll two tubes of crescent roll dough; separate into rectangles. Place rectangles in an ungreased 15-in. x 10-in. x 1-in. baking pan. Press onto the bottom and 1/4 in. up the sides of pan to form a crust, sealing seams and perforations. Bake at 375° for 5-7 minutes or until light golden brown.

In a bowl, combine the turkey, cheese, broccoli, soup, milk, mustard, onion, salt and pepper; mix well. Spoon over crust. Unroll remaining dough; divide into rectangles. Seal perforations. Cut each rectangle into four 1-in. strips. Using strips, make a lattice design on top of turkey mixture. Brush with egg. Bake 17-22 minutes longer or until top crust is golden brown and filling is hot. **Yield:** 12-16 servings.

Home-Style Roast Beef

(Pictured above)

Sandra Furman-Krajewski
Amsterdam, New York

A very moist roast, this gains richness from the gravy, and the bacon gives it a somewhat different taste. For variety, you can cube the roast and serve it over rice with gravy...or cube and mix it with noodles, gravy and vegetables if you'd like to make it into a casserole.

    1 bottom round beef roast (10 to 12 pounds)
    1 can (14-1/2 ounces) chicken broth
    1 can (10-1/4 ounces) beef gravy
    1 can (10-3/4 ounces) condensed cream of
      celery soup, undiluted
  1/4 cup water
  1/4 cup Worcestershire sauce
  1/4 cup soy sauce
    3 tablespoons dried parsley flakes
    3 tablespoons dill weed
    2 tablespoons dried thyme
4-1/2 teaspoons garlic powder
    1 teaspoon celery salt
Pepper to taste
    1 large onion, sliced 1/4 inch thick
    8 bacon strips
  1/4 cup butter *or* margarine, cut into cubes

Place roast in a large roasting pan with fat side up. Prick meat in several places with a meat fork. Combine broth, gravy, soup, water, Worcestershire sauce and soy sauce; pour over roast. Sprinkle with seasonings. Arrange onion slices over roast. Place bacon strips diagonally over onion. Dot with butter.

Bake, uncovered, at 325° for 2-1/2 to 3-1/2 hours or until the meat reaches desired doneness (for rare, a meat thermometer should read 140°; medium, 160°; well-done, 170°). Let stand for 15 minutes before slicing. **Yield:** 25-30 servings.

Chicken Broccoli Lasagna

(Pictured above)

Lisa Reilly, Kingston, Massachusetts

My family prefers this tasty chicken dish over a more traditional lasagna.

    6 tablespoons butter *or* margarine, *divided*
  1/4 cup all-purpose flour
    2 cups milk
    1 cup chicken broth
    3 eggs, beaten
  3/4 cup grated Parmesan cheese, *divided*
    1 teaspoon salt, *divided*
Pinch ground nutmeg
Pinch cayenne pepper
    1 cup chopped onion
    1 garlic clove, minced
    2 cups diced cooked chicken
    1 package (16 ounces) frozen chopped broccoli, thawed and drained
  1/2 cup shredded carrot
  1/4 cup minced fresh parsley
  1/4 teaspoon pepper
  15 lasagna noodles, cooked and drained
    4 cups (16 ounces) shredded mozzarella cheese

In a saucepan, melt 4 tablespoons butter; stir in flour until smooth. Gradually add milk and broth; bring to a boil. Boil and stir for 2 minutes. Whisk half into eggs; return all to pan. Cook and stir over low heat for about 1 minute or until mixture reaches at least 160°. Remove from heat; add 1/2 cup Parmesan, 1/2 teaspoon salt, nutmeg and cayenne. Set aside.

In a skillet, saute onion and garlic in remaining butter until tender. Add chicken, broccoli, carrot, parsley, pepper and remaining salt; cook for 3 minutes. Spread 1/2 cup of the Parmesan custard mixture into an ungreased 13-in. x 9-in. x 2-in. baking dish. Layer with a third of the noodles, half of the chicken mixture, 1/2 cup Parmesan custard, a third of the mozzarella cheese and 1 tablespoon Parmesan cheese. Repeat layers. Top with re-

maining noodles, mozzarella and Parmesan custard. Sprinkle with remaining Parmesan cheese. Bake, uncovered, at 350° for 40-45 minutes or until bubbly. Let stand 10 minutes before serving. **Yield:** 12 servings.

Michigan Beans and Sausage

(Pictured below)

Janice Lass, Dorr, Michigan

I got this recipe from a church cookbook years ago. Bean casseroles like this one are always a big hit at potlucks and picnics.

    1 pound fully cooked kielbasa *or* Polish sausage, halved lengthwise and thinly sliced
    1 medium onion, chopped
    1 cup ketchup
  3/4 cup packed brown sugar
  1/2 cup sugar
    2 tablespoons vinegar
    2 tablespoons molasses
    2 tablespoons prepared mustard
    3 cans (15-1/2 ounces *each*) great northern beans, rinsed and drained

In a saucepan, cook sausage and onion in boiling water for 2 minutes; drain. In a bowl, combine the ketchup, sugars, vinegar, molasses and mustard. Stir in the beans and sausage mixture. Transfer to a greased 2-1/2-qt. baking dish. Cover and bake at 350° for 1-1/2 hours or until bean mixture reaches desired thickness. **Yield:** 14-16 servings.

Editor's Note: This recipe can also be prepared in a slow cooker. Prepare as directed, transferring to a slow cooker instead of a baking dish. Cover and cook on low for 6-8 hours or until heated through.

Tarragon Chicken Casserole

Bob Breno, Strongsville, Ohio

For a quick and hearty main dish that's ideal when the weather's warm, try this casserole. Calling for chicken that's already cooked, it bakes in just half an hour. People always tell me that they love the tasty sauce and cheese on top.

- 2 cans (10-3/4 ounces *each*) condensed cream of chicken soup, undiluted
- 2 cups half-and-half cream
- 4 teaspoons dried tarragon
- 1/2 teaspoon pepper
- 1 package (16 ounces) linguine *or* spaghetti, cooked and drained
- 6 cups cubed cooked chicken
- 1/2 cup grated Parmesan cheese

Paprika, optional

In a large bowl, combine soup, cream, tarragon and pepper. Stir in the linguine and chicken. Transfer to an ungreased 4-qt. baking dish. Sprinkle with the Parmesan cheese and paprika if desired. Bake, uncovered, at 350° for 30 minutes or until heated through. **Yield:** 12 servings.

Corn Dog Casserole

Marcy Suzanne Olipane
Belleville, Illinois

Reminiscent of traditional corn dogs on a stick, this fun-to-eat main dish really hits the spot, especially on cool fall days. It's perfect for the football parties my husband and I often host. Guests always go back for seconds and thirds. The casserole tastes especially good right from the oven.

- 2 cups thinly sliced celery
- 2 tablespoons butter *or* margarine
- 1-1/2 cups sliced green onions
- 1-1/2 pounds hot dogs
- 2 eggs
- 1-1/2 cups milk
- 2 teaspoons rubbed sage
- 1/4 teaspoon pepper
- 2 packages (8-1/2 ounces *each*) corn bread/ muffin mix
- 2 cups (8 ounces) shredded sharp cheddar cheese, *divided*

In a skillet, saute celery in butter for 5 minutes. Add onions; saute for 5 minutes. Place in a large bowl; set aside. Cut hot dogs lengthwise into quarters, then cut into thirds. In the same skillet, saute the hot dogs for 5 minutes or until lightly browned; add to vegetables. Set aside 1 cup.

In a large bowl, combine the eggs, milk, sage and pepper. Add the remaining hot dog mixture. Stir in corn bread mixes. Add 1-1/2 cups of cheddar cheese. Spread into a shallow 3-qt. baking dish. Top with reserved hot dog mixture and remaining cheese. Bake, uncovered, at 400° for 30 minutes or until golden brown. **Yield:** 12 servings.

Chicken Noodle Casserole

(Pictured above)

Cheryl Watts, Natural Bridge, Virginia

This tasty dish gets even better after it's been refrigerated a day or two, so the leftovers are always great. We eat it hot in the winter and cold in the summer.

- 1 package (16 ounces) egg noodles
- 1 medium sweet red pepper, chopped
- 1 large onion, chopped
- 1 celery rib, chopped
- 2 garlic cloves, minced
- 1/4 cup butter *or* margarine
- 1-1/2 cups sliced fresh mushrooms
- 3 tablespoons all-purpose flour
- 3 cups chicken broth
- 3 cups half-and-half cream
- 2 packages (8 ounces *each*) cream cheese, cubed
- 12 cups cubed cooked chicken
- 1 to 1-1/2 teaspoons salt

TOPPING:
- 1 cup finely crushed cornflakes
- 2 tablespoons butter *or* margarine, melted
- 1 tablespoon vegetable oil
- 3 tablespoons minced fresh parsley
- 1/2 teaspoon paprika

Cook noodles according to package directions; drain. In a large skillet, saute the red pepper, onion, celery and garlic in butter until tender. Add mushrooms; cook 1-2 minutes longer or until tender. Remove vegetables with a slotted spoon; set aside. Add flour to the skillet; stir until blended. Gradually add broth. Bring to a boil; cook and stir for 2 minutes or until thickened. Reduce heat. Gradually stir in cream. Add the cream cheese; cook and stir until cheese is melted. Remove from the heat.

In a large bowl, combine the chicken, salt, noodles, vegetables and cheese sauce; mix well. Transfer to two ungreased shallow 3-qt. baking dishes. Combine topping ingredients. Sprinkle over top. Cover and bake at 350° for 20 minutes. Uncover; bake 15-20 minutes longer or until hot and bubbly. **Yield:** 2 casseroles (8-10 servings each).

Turkey Croquettes with Cranberry Salsa

(Pictured below)

Jacque Capurro, Anchorage, Alaska

This recipe is a great way to use up leftover turkey after the holidays.

- 1/3 cup chopped onion
- 2 tablespoons butter *or* margarine
- 1/4 cup all-purpose flour
- 1/4 cup milk
- 1/4 cup chicken broth
- 2 cups finely chopped cooked turkey
- 1/2 cup mashed sweet potato
- 1/2 teaspoon salt
- 1/4 teaspoon pepper
- 1/8 teaspoon cayenne pepper

SALSA:
- 3/4 cup chopped tart green apple
- 1 tablespoon lemon juice
- 1/2 cup chopped cranberries
- 2 green onions, chopped
- 2 jalapeno peppers, seeded and chopped*
- 3 tablespoons golden raisins, chopped
- 1 tablespoon honey

CROQUETTES:
- 2 eggs
- 1 tablespoon water
- 1/2 cup all-purpose flour
- 1/2 cup dry bread crumbs
- Oil for deep-fat frying

In a saucepan, saute onion in butter until tender. Stir in flour until blended. Gradually add milk and broth. Bring to a boil; cook and stir for 2 minutes or until thickened. Remove from the heat; stir in turkey, sweet potato, salt, pepper and cayenne. Cover and refrigerate for 2 hours or until firm.

Meanwhile, toss apple with lemon juice in a bowl. Stir in remaining salsa ingredients. Cover and chill for at least 1 hour. For croquettes, beat eggs and water in a shallow bowl. Place flour and bread crumbs in separate shallow bowls. Shape turkey mixture into 1-1/2-in. balls. Roll in flour; shake off excess. Roll in egg mixture, then in crumbs. In an electric skillet or deep-fat fryer, heat 1-1/2 in. of oil to 375°. Fry croquettes, a few at a time, for 2 minutes or until golden brown. Drain on paper towels. Serve with cranberry salsa. **Yield:** 16 croquettes (2 cups salsa).

*Editor's Note: When cutting or seeding hot peppers, use rubber or plastic gloves to protect your hands. Avoid touching your face.

Prairie Meat Loaf

Karen Laubman, Spruce Grove, Alberta

You can't top a hearty helping of meat loaf with creamy mashed potatoes on the side. This tender, moist meat loaf with a hint of cheese is a big hit at our house. The addition of oats boosts its nutritional value.

- 2 eggs
- 1/2 cup ketchup
- 2 tablespoons prepared mustard
- 3 cups old-fashioned oats
- 2 teaspoons salt
- 1 teaspoon garlic powder
- 1 teaspoon dried thyme
- 1 teaspoon dried basil
- 1-1/2 cups beef broth
- 1-1/2 cups finely chopped onion
- 1-1/2 cups finely chopped celery
- 2-1/2 cups (10 ounces) shredded cheddar cheese, *divided*
- 4 pounds lean ground beef

In a large bowl, beat eggs; stir in ketchup, mustard, oats, salt, garlic powder, thyme and basil. In a small saucepan, bring broth to a boil; add to oat mixture and mix well. Stir in onion, celery and 2 cups of cheese. Add beef; mix well. Press into two ungreased 9-in. x 5-in. x 3-in. loaf pans. Bake at 375° for 1-1/4 hours or until a meat thermometer reads 170° and juices run clear; drain. Sprinkle with remaining cheese; let stand until melted. **Yield**: 2 loaves (6-8 servings each).

Polish Reuben Casserole

Imogene Peterson, Ontario, Oregon

People are always asking me for this recipe. It's easy to assemble and great to take to potlucks, which we have a lot of in our farming community.

- 1 package (8 ounces) egg noodles
- 2 cans (14 ounces *each*) Bavarian sauerkraut, drained
- 2 cans (10-3/4 ounces *each*) condensed cream of mushroom soup, undiluted
- 1-1/3 cups milk
- 1 medium onion, chopped
- 1 tablespoon prepared mustard
- 1-1/2 pounds Polish sausage *or* kielbasa, halved and cut into 1/2-inch slices
- 2 cups (8 ounces) shredded Swiss cheese
- 1/2 cup soft rye bread crumbs
- 2 tablespoons butter *or* margarine, melted

Cook noodles according to package directions; drain. Spread sauerkraut in a greased shallow 4-qt. baking dish. Top with noodles. In a bowl, combine the soup, milk, onion and mustard; pour over the noodles. Top with sausage; sprinkle with cheese. Combine bread crumbs and butter; sprinkle over the top. Cover and bake at 350° for 30-35 minutes or until heated through. **Yield:** 12-14 servings.

Sausage Noodle Casserole

(Pictured below)

Julia Livingston, Frostproof, Florida

The sausage makes this casserole meaty and hearty, and the blue cheese adds a special flavor. It's easy to prepare, plus it only needs to bake for about 30 minutes.

- 1 package (16 ounces) egg noodles
- 2 pounds bulk pork sausage
- 2 cans (10-3/4 ounces *each*) condensed cream of chicken soup, undiluted
- 2 cups (16 ounces) sour cream
- 1 cup crumbled blue cheese
- 2 jars (4-1/2 ounces *each*) sliced mushrooms, drained
- 1 jar (4 ounces) diced pimientos, drained
- 1/4 cup finely chopped green pepper
- 1 cup soft bread crumbs
- 2 tablespoons butter *or* margarine, melted

Cook noodles according to package directions; drain. In a large skillet, cook sausage over medium heat until no longer pink; drain.

In a Dutch oven, combine the soup, sour cream and blue cheese; cook and stir over medium heat until cheese is melted. Stir in the noodles, sausage, mushrooms, pimientos and green pepper. Transfer to two greased 3-qt. baking dishes. Toss bread crumbs and butter; sprinkle over top. Bake, uncovered, at 350° for 30-35 minutes or until edges are bubbly. **Yield:** 2 casseroles (8 servings each).

Beef Burritos

(Pictured above)

Amy Martin, Waddell, Arizona

Living in Arizona, we enjoy all sorts of foods with Southwestern flair, such as these beef-stuffed tortillas. The recipe is both easy to make and easy to serve—folks can assemble their own burritos with their choice of garnishes.

- 2 chuck pot roasts (2-1/2 to 3 pounds *each*)
- 2 tablespoons vegetable oil
- 1 cup water
- 1 large onion, chopped
- 4 garlic cloves, minced
- 2 teaspoons dried oregano
- 2 teaspoons salt
- 1 teaspoon pepper
- 1 can (28 ounces) diced tomatoes, undrained
- 2 cans (4 ounces *each*) chopped green chilies
- 2 tablespoons all-purpose flour
- 1/4 cup cold water
- 4 to 6 drops hot pepper sauce
- 18 flour tortillas (8 inches), warmed

Shredded cheddar cheese, sour cream and salsa

In a Dutch oven over medium heat, brown roasts in oil; drain. Add water, onion, garlic, oregano, salt and pepper; bring to a boil. Reduce heat; cover and simmer for 2 to 2-1/2 hours or until meat is tender. Remove roasts; cool. Remove meat from bone and cut into bite-size pieces. Skim fat from pan juices. Add tomatoes and chilies; mix well. Add meat; bring to a boil. Reduce heat; simmer, uncovered, for 30 minutes.

Combine the flour and cold water; mix well. Stir into the beef mixture. Cook over medium heat, stirring constantly, until thickened and bubbly. Add the hot pepper sauce. Spoon down the center of tortillas; fold top and bottom of tortilla over filling and roll up. Serve with cheese, sour cream and salsa. **Yield:** 18 servings.

Hearty Meat Pie

(Pictured below)

Twila Burkholder, Middleburg, Pennsylvania

Use prepared pie crust to speed preparation of this homemade meat and vegetable pie topped with a tasty mushroom gravy.

Pastry for two double-crust pies
   2 cups grated peeled potatoes
1-1/4 cups diced celery
   1 cup grated carrots
   1/4 cup chopped onion
   2 tablespoons Worcestershire sauce
   1 teaspoon salt
   1/4 teaspoon pepper
   3/4 pound uncooked lean ground beef
MUSHROOM GRAVY (for each pie):
   1 can (4 ounces) mushroom stems and pieces
   2 tablespoons all-purpose flour
   2 tablespoons vegetable oil
   1 teaspoon beef bouillon granules
   4 drops browning sauce, optional

Divide pastry into fourths. On a lightly floured surface, roll out one portion to fit a 9-in. pie plate. In a bowl, combine the next seven ingredients; add beef and mix well. Spoon half into crust. Roll out another portion of pastry to fit top of pie; place over filling and seal edges. Cut vents in top pastry. Repeat with remaining pastry and filling. Cover and freeze one pie for up to 3 months. Bake second pie at 375° for 15 minutes. Reduce heat; bake at 350° for 1 hour.

Meanwhile, drain the mushrooms, reserving liquid. Add water to liquid to measure 1 cup; set aside. In a saucepan, cook the mushrooms and flour in oil until bubbly. Remove from the heat; stir in the bouillon and reserved mushroom liquid. Bring to a boil; cook and stir for 1 minute. Stir in browning sauce if desired. Serve with meat pie. To use frozen meat pie: Bake at 375° for 70 minutes. Make gravy as directed. **Yield:** 2 pies (6-8 servings each).

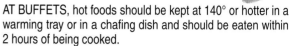

Potluck Pointer

AT BUFFETS, hot foods should be kept at 140° or hotter in a warming tray or in a chafing dish and should be eaten within 2 hours of being cooked.

Cold foods should be kept at 40° or colder. When setting out cold foods, consider placing the serving containers in a larger pan filled with ice to keep them cold.

Hawaiian Pizza Pasta

Rose Enns, Abbotsford, British Columbia

I've been making this recipe since I discovered it and tweaked it to our family's liking more than 15 years ago. You can substitute chopped salami, pepperoni or cooked ground beef for the ham. Or add olives, red peppers—whatever you like on a pizza.

   1/2 pound fresh mushrooms, sliced
   1 medium onion, chopped
   1 medium green pepper, chopped
   2 garlic cloves, minced
   3 tablespoons vegetable oil
   1 can (15 ounces) tomato sauce
   2 bay leaves
   1 teaspoon dried oregano
   1 teaspoon dried basil
1/2 teaspoon sugar
3-1/2 cups uncooked spiral pasta
   6 cups (24 ounces) shredded mozzarella cheese, *divided*
   1 can (20 ounces) pineapple chunks, drained
   1 cup cubed fully cooked ham

In a large saucepan, saute the mushrooms, onion, green pepper and garlic in oil for 5 minutes or until tender. Add the tomato sauce, bay leaves, oregano, basil and sugar. Bring to a boil. Reduce heat; simmer, uncovered, for 20-30 minutes or until thickened, stirring frequently. Meanwhile, cook pasta according to package directions; drain.

Discard bay leaves from sauce. Add pasta, 5 cups of mozzarella cheese, pineapple and ham. Transfer to a greased shallow 3-qt. baking dish. Sprinkle with remaining cheese. Bake, uncovered, at 350° for 30-35 minutes or until heated through. **Yield:** 12-14 servings.

Pork Carnitas

Tracy Byers, Corvallis, Oregon

I use this recipe often when entertaining. I set out all the toppings, and folks have fun assembling their own carnitas. Because I can prepare everything in advance, I get to spend more time with my guests.

   1 boneless pork shoulder *or* loin roast (2 to 3 pounds), trimmed and cut into 3-inch cubes
1/2 cup lime juice
   1 teaspoon salt

> 1/2 teaspoon pepper
> 1/2 teaspoon crushed red pepper flakes
> 12 flour tortillas (7 inches), warmed
> 2 cups (8 ounces) shredded cheddar *or* Monterey Jack cheese
> 2 medium avocados, peeled and diced
> 2 medium tomatoes, diced
> 1 medium onion, diced
> Shredded lettuce
> Minced fresh cilantro, optional
> Salsa

In a slow cooker, combine pork, lime juice, salt, pepper and pepper flakes. Cover and cook on high for 1 hour; stir. Reduce heat to low and cook 8-10 hours longer or until meat is very tender. Shred pork with a fork (it may look somewhat pink).

Spoon about 1/3 cup of filling down the center of each tortilla; top with cheese, avocados, tomatoes, onion, lettuce and cilantro if desired. Fold in bottom and sides of tortilla. Serve with salsa. **Yield:** 12 servings.

Special Ham Slices

(Pictured below)

The taste-tempting sauce topping these ham slices was developed by our Test Kitchen. It deliciously combines orange juice, brown sugar and spices and gives a wonderful flavor to the ham.

> 12 boneless ham steaks (about 3 pounds)
> 1 cup orange juice
> 3/4 cup packed brown sugar
> 2 teaspoons grated orange peel
> 1 teaspoon ground mustard
> 1/4 teaspoon ground cloves

Place ham in an ungreased 13-in. x 9-in. x 2-in. baking dish. Combine remaining ingredients; pour over ham. Bake, uncovered, at 325° for 20-25 minutes or until heated through, basting occasionally. **Yield:** 12 servings.

Baked Spaghetti

(Pictured above)

Ruth Koberna, Brecksville, Ohio

Every time that I make this cheesy dish, I get requests for the recipe. It puts a different spin on spaghetti and is great for any meal.

> 1 cup chopped onion
> 1 cup chopped green pepper
> 1 tablespoon butter *or* margarine
> 1 can (28 ounces) diced tomatoes, undrained
> 1 can (4 ounces) mushroom stems and pieces, drained
> 1 can (2-1/4 ounces) sliced ripe olives, drained
> 2 teaspoons dried oregano
> 1 pound ground beef, browned and drained, optional
> 12 ounces spaghetti, cooked and drained
> 2 cups (8 ounces) shredded cheddar cheese
> 1 can (10-3/4 ounces) condensed cream of mushroom soup, undiluted
> 1/4 cup water
> 1/4 cup grated Parmesan cheese

In a large skillet, saute onion and green pepper in butter until tender. Add tomatoes, mushrooms, olives and oregano. Add ground beef if desired. Simmer, uncovered, for 10 minutes.

Place half of the spaghetti in a greased 13-in. x 9-in. x 2-in. baking dish. Top with half of the vegetable mixture. Sprinkle with 1 cup of cheddar cheese. Repeat layers. Mix the soup and water until smooth; pour over casserole. Sprinkle with Parmesan cheese. Bake, uncovered, at 350° for 30-35 minutes or until heated through. **Yield:** 12 servings.

Breads, Rolls & Muffins

Golden Crescents (p. 69)

Chapter 6

Herbed Oatmeal Pan Bread

(Pictured below)

Karen Bourne, Magrath, Alberta

This beautiful, golden pan bread is especially good with a steaming bowl of homemade soup.

- 1-1/2 cups boiling water
- 1 cup old-fashioned oats
- 2 packages (1/4 ounce *each*) active dry yeast
- 1/2 cup warm water (110° to 115°)
- 1/4 cup sugar
- 3 tablespoons butter *or* margarine, softened
- 2 teaspoons salt
- 1 egg, lightly beaten
- 4 to 4-3/4 cups all-purpose flour

TOPPING:
- 1/4 cup butter *or* margarine, melted, *divided*
- 2 tablespoons grated Parmesan cheese
- 1 teaspoon dried basil
- 1/2 teaspoon dried oregano
- 1/2 teaspoon garlic powder

In a small bowl, combine boiling water and oats; cool to lukewarm (110° to 115°). In a mixing bowl, dissolve yeast in warm water. Add sugar, butter, salt, egg, oat mixture and 2 cups of flour; beat until smooth. Add enough remaining flour to form a soft dough.

Turn onto a floured surface; knead until smooth and elastic, about 6-8 minutes. Place in a greased bowl, turning once to grease top. Cover and let rise in a warm place until doubled, about 30 minutes.

Punch dough down and press evenly into a greased 13-in. x 9-in. x 2-in. baking pan. With a very sharp knife, cut diagonal lines 1-1/2 in. apart completely through dough. Repeat in opposite direction, creating a diamond pattern. Cover and let rise in a warm place until doubled, about 1 hour. Redefine pattern by gently poking along cut lines with knife tip. Brush with 2 tablespoons melted butter. Bake at 375° for 15 minutes.

Meanwhile, combine Parmesan cheese, basil, oregano and garlic powder. Brush bread with remaining butter; sprinkle with cheese mixture. Bake for 5 minutes. Loosely cover with foil and bake 5 minutes longer. Serve warm. **Yield:** 8-10 servings.

Beautiful Brown Rolls

Anna Anderson, Atwater, Minnesota

I love to make bread and have baked many, many dozens of these rolls over the years. Everyone agrees these light-textured rolls are outstanding.

- 2 cups boiling water
- 1 cup quick-cooking oats
- 2 packages (1/4 ounce *each*) active dry yeast
- 1/4 cup warm water (110° to 115°)
- 2 eggs, beaten
- 1/2 cup molasses
- 1/2 cup vegetable oil
- 1/3 cup sugar
- 1/2 teaspoon salt
- 5-3/4 to 6-1/4 cups all-purpose flour
- Melted butter *or* margarine

In a large mixing bowl, combine boiling water and oats; cool to lukewarm (110° to 115°). Meanwhile, dissolve yeast in warm water; stir into oat mixture. Add the eggs, molasses, oil, sugar and salt. Add enough flour to form a soft dough.

Turn onto a floured surface; knead until smooth and elastic, about 6-8 minutes. Place in a greased bowl, turning once to grease top. Cover and let rise in a warm place until doubled, about 1 hour.

Punch dough down. Divide into 36 pieces and shape into rolls. Place on greased baking sheets. Cover and let rise until doubled, about 30 minutes. Bake at 375° for 20-25 minutes. Brush with butter. Cool on wire racks. **Yield:** 3 dozen.

Herbed Peasant Bread

Ardath Effa, Villa Park, Illinois

The recipe for this beautiful flavorful loaf came from our daughter-in-law, Karen. She's a great cook. Everyone who enjoys a slice of this moist bread asks me for a copy of the recipe.

- 1/2 cup chopped onion
- 3 tablespoons butter *or* margarine
- 1 cup plus 2 tablespoons warm milk (120° to 130°)
- 1 tablespoon sugar
- 1-1/2 teaspoons salt
- 1/2 teaspoon dill weed
- 1/2 teaspoon dried basil
- 1/2 teaspoon dried rosemary, crushed
- 1 package (1/4 ounce) active dry yeast
- 3 to 3-1/2 cups all-purpose flour
- Melted butter *or* margarine

In a skillet over low heat, saute onion in butter until tender, about 8 minutes. Cool for 10 minutes. Place in a mixing bowl. Add milk, sugar, salt, herbs, yeast and 3 cups flour; beat until smooth. Add enough remaining flour to form a soft dough.

Turn onto a floured surface; knead until smooth and elastic, about 6-8 minutes. Place in a greased bowl, turning once to grease top. Cover and let rise in a warm place until doubled, about 45 minutes.

Punch the dough down. Shape into a ball and place on a greased baking sheet. Cover and let rise until doubled, about 45 minutes. Bake at 375° for 25-30 minutes. Remove to a wire rack; brush with melted butter. Cool. **Yield:** 1 loaf.

Lemon Cheese Braid

(Pictured below)

Grace Dickey, Vernonia, Oregon

This bread always gets rave reviews. Although fairly simple to make, when you finish you'll feel a sense of accomplishment because it tastes delicious.

1 package (1/4 ounce) active dry yeast
3 tablespoons warm water (110° to 115°)
1/4 cup sugar
1/3 cup milk
1/4 cup butter *or* margarine, melted
2 eggs
1/2 teaspoon salt
3 to 3-1/2 cups all-purpose flour
FILLING:
2 packages (one 8 ounces, one 3 ounces)
**   cream cheese, softened**
1/2 cup sugar
1 egg
1 teaspoon grated lemon peel
ICING:
1/2 cup confectioners' sugar
2 to 3 teaspoons milk
1/4 teaspoon vanilla extract

In a mixing bowl, dissolve yeast in warm water; let stand for 5 minutes. Add sugar, milk, butter, eggs, salt and 2 cups flour; beat on low speed for 3 minutes. Stir in enough of the remaining flour to form a soft dough.

Turn onto a floured surface; knead until smooth and elastic, about 6-8 minutes. Place in a greased bowl, turning once to grease top. Cover and let rise in a warm place until doubled, about 1 hour. Meanwhile, beat filling ingredients in a mixing bowl until fluffy; set aside.

Punch dough down. On a floured surface, roll into a 14-in. x 12-in. rectangle. Place on a greased baking sheet. Spread filling down center third of rectangle. On each long side, cut 1-in.-wide strips, 3 in. into center. Starting at one end, fold alternating strips at an angle across filling. Seal end. Cover and let rise for 30 minutes. Bake at 375° for 25-30 minutes or until golden brown. Cool. Combine icing ingredients; drizzle over bread. **Yield:** 12-14 servings.

Soft Breadsticks

(Pictured above)

Nancy Johnson, Connersville, Indiana

I've been making these tasty breadsticks that go with almost any meal for years. Since they use ingredients like flour, sugar, baking powder and milk, it's convenient and inexpensive to mix up a batch.

1-1/4 cups all-purpose flour
2 teaspoons sugar
1-1/2 teaspoons baking powder
1/2 teaspoon salt
2/3 cup milk
3 tablespoons butter *or* margarine, melted
2 teaspoons sesame seeds

In a small bowl, combine flour, sugar, baking powder and salt. Gradually add milk and stir to form a soft dough. Turn onto a floured surface; knead gently 3-4 times. Roll into a 10-in. x 5-in. x 1/2-in. rectangle; cut into 12 breadsticks.

Place butter in a 13-in. x 9-in. x 2-in. baking pan. Place breadsticks in the butter and turn to coat. Sprinkle with sesame seeds. Bake at 450° for 14-18 minutes or until golden brown. Serve warm. **Yield:** 1 dozen.

Green Chili Corn Muffins

Melissa Cook, Chico, California

While visiting a local Mexican restaurant, I sampled a spicy corn muffin with a surprising sweetness. This recipe is a result of numerous attempts to re-create that treat using convenient mixes. These moist muffins are tasty with Mexican dishes, chili and soup.

    1 package (8-1/2 ounces) corn bread/muffin mix
    1 package (9 ounces) yellow cake mix
    2 eggs
1/2 cup milk
1/3 cup water
    2 tablespoons vegetable oil
    1 can (4 ounces) chopped green chilies, drained
    1 cup (4 ounces) shredded cheddar cheese, *divided*

In a bowl, combine dry corn bread and cake mixes. In another bowl, combine the eggs, milk, water and oil. Stir into the dry ingredients just until moistened. Add chilies and 3/4 cup cheese. Fill greased or paper-lined muffin cups two-thirds full. Bake at 350° for 20-22 minutes or until muffins test done. Immediately sprinkle with remaining cheese. Cool for 5 minutes before removing from pans to wire racks. Serve warm. **Yield:** 16 servings.

Yogurt Yeast Rolls

(Pictured above)

Carol Forcum, Marion, Illinois

People tend to snap up these fluffy, golden rolls in a hurry whenever I take them to a potluck. It's a nice contribution since rolls are easy to transport and one batch goes a long way.

1-1/2 cups whole wheat flour
3-1/4 cups all-purpose flour, *divided*
    2 packages (1/4 ounce *each*) active dry yeast
    2 teaspoons salt
1/2 teaspoon baking soda
1-1/2 cups (12 ounces) plain yogurt
1/2 cup water
    3 tablespoons butter *or* margarine
    2 tablespoons honey

In a mixing bowl, combine whole wheat flour, 1/2 cup all-purpose flour, yeast, salt and baking soda. In a saucepan over low heat, heat the yogurt, water, butter and honey to 120°-130°. Pour over the dry ingredients; blend well. Beat on medium speed for 3 minutes. Add enough remaining all-purpose flour to form a soft dough.

Turn onto a floured surface; knead until smooth and elastic, about 6-8 minutes. Place in a greased bowl, turning once to grease top. Cover and let rise in a warm place until doubled, about 1 hour. Punch dough down; divide into 24 pieces.

Roll each piece into a 9-in. rope. To form S-shaped rolls, coil each end of rope toward center in opposite directions. Place 3 in. apart on greased baking sheets. Cover and let rise until doubled, about 30 minutes. Bake at 400° for 15 minutes or until golden brown. Spray tops with nonstick cooking spray while warm. Cool on wire racks. **Yield:** 2 dozen.

Onion Mustard Buns

**Melodie Shumaker
Elizabethtown, Pennsylvania**

I'm an avid bread baker and was thrilled to find this recipe. It makes delectably different rolls that are a hit wherever I take them. They are special enough to serve alongside an elaborate main dish.

✓ Uses less fat, sugar or salt. Includes Nutritional Analysis and Diabetic Exchanges.

    1 package (1/4 ounce) active dry yeast
1/4 cup warm water (110° to 115°)
    2 cups warm milk (110° to 115°)
    3 tablespoons dried minced onion
    3 tablespoons prepared mustard
    2 tablespoons vegetable oil
    2 tablespoons sugar
1-1/2 teaspoons salt
    6 to 6-1/2 cups all-purpose flour

In a mixing bowl, dissolve yeast in water. Add milk, onion, mustard, oil, sugar, salt and 4 cups flour; beat until smooth. Add enough remaining flour to form a soft dough.

Turn onto a floured surface; knead until smooth and elastic, about 6-8 minutes. Place in a greased bowl, turning once to grease top. Cover and let rise in a warm place until doubled, about 1 hour.

Punch dough down; divide into 24 pieces. Flatten each piece into a 3-in. circle. Place 1 in. apart on greased baking sheets. Cover and let rise until doubled, about 45 minutes. Bake at 350° for 20-25 minutes or until golden brown. Cool on wire racks. **Yield:** 2 dozen.

Nutritional Analysis: One bun (prepared with skim

milk) equals 138 calories, 181 mg sodium, trace cholesterol, 26 gm carbohydrate, 4 gm protein, 2 gm fat. **Diabetic Exchanges:** 1-1/2 starch, 1/2 fat.

Golden Crescents

(Pictured below)

Bertha Johnson, Indianapolis, Indiana

My family requests these rolls for every Sunday dinner. Pulling their share of these slightly sweet, tender rolls from out of the basket, my grandchildren look at me and say, "Grandma, you are the world's best cook."

- 2 packages (1/4 ounce *each*) active dry yeast
- 3/4 cup warm water (110° to 115°)
- 1/2 cup sugar
- 1/4 cup plus 2 tablespoons butter *or* margarine, softened, *divided*
- 2 tablespoons shortening
- 2 eggs
- 1 teaspoon salt
- 4 to 4-1/2 cups all-purpose flour
- Additional butter *or* margarine, melted, optional

In a mixing bowl, dissolve yeast in water. Add sugar, 1/4 cup butter, shortening, eggs, salt and 2 cups flour; beat until smooth. Add enough of the remaining flour to form a soft dough.

Turn onto a floured surface; knead until smooth and elastic, about 6-8 minutes. Place in a greased bowl, turning once to grease top. Cover and let rise in a warm place until doubled, about 1-1/2 hours.

Punch the dough down; divide in half. Roll each portion into a 12-in. circle. Melt remaining butter; brush over dough. Cut each circle into 12 wedges. Roll up wedges from the wide end and curve to form crescents. Place with point down 2 in. apart on greased baking sheets.

Cover and let rise until doubled, about 45 minutes. Bake at 375° for 8-10 minutes or until golden brown. Brush with butter if desired. **Yield:** 2 dozen.

English Muffin Loaves

(Pictured above)

Roberta Freedman, Mesilla Park, New Mexico

Slices of these festive fruit and nut loaves are a terrific breakfast on a cold morning. They have a subtle cornmeal flavor. The best part is that no kneading is required. I serve one loaf right from the oven and freeze the other or give it as a gift.

- 5 cups all-purpose flour, *divided*
- 2 packages (1/4 ounce *each*) active dry yeast
- 2 tablespoons sugar
- 2 teaspoons ground cinnamon
- 1 teaspoon salt
- 1/4 teaspoon baking soda
- 1-1/2 cups warm orange juice (120° to 130°)
- 1/2 cup warm water (120° to 130°)
- 1/4 cup vegetable oil
- 1/2 cup chopped pecans
- 1/2 cup chopped dried apricots
- Cornmeal

In a mixing bowl, combine 2 cups flour, yeast, sugar, cinnamon, salt and baking soda. Add orange juice, water and oil; beat on low speed until moistened. Beat on high for 3 minutes. Stir in the pecans, apricots and remaining flour to form a stiff batter. Do not knead.

Grease two 8-in. x 4-in. x 2-in. loaf pans; sprinkle with cornmeal. Spoon batter into pans; sprinkle with cornmeal. Cover and let rise in a warm place until doubled, about 45 minutes. Bake at 350° for 35-40 minutes or until golden brown. Immediately remove from pans to cool on wire racks. Slice and toast. **Yield:** 2 loaves.

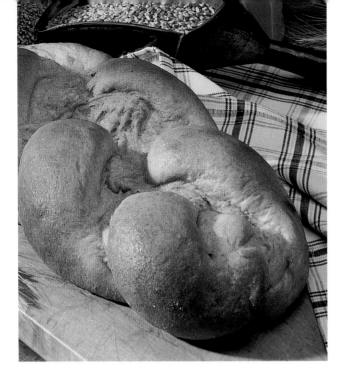

Fruit 'n' Nut Mini Loaves

Judi Oudekerk, Buffalo, Minnesota

My family really enjoys these pretty mini loaves—every slice is loaded with fruit and nuts. You can substitute dates for the dried apricots...or use red and green maraschino cherries at Christmas for added color.

```
1-1/2 cups all-purpose flour
1-1/2 cups sugar
    1 teaspoon baking powder
  1/2 teaspoon salt
    1 pound dried apricots or dates, halved
    1 pound Brazil nuts
    1 cup pecan halves
    1 jar (10 ounces) maraschino cherries, drained
    5 eggs
    1 teaspoon vanilla extract
```

In a large bowl, combine the dry ingredients. Add apricots, nuts and cherries; mix well. Beat eggs and vanilla; stir into the dry ingredients just until moistened.

Spoon into eight greased and floured 4-1/2-in. x 2-1/2-in. x 1-1/2-in. loaf pans (pans will be full). Bake at 325° for 40-50 minutes or until a toothpick inserted near the center comes out clean. Cool for 10 minutes; remove from the pans to wire racks. Cool completely before slicing. **Yield:** 8 mini loaves.

Cheese Twists

(Pictured above)

Michelle Beran, Claflin, Kansas

These impressive loaves take a little time to prepare, but they're well worth the effort. I love making bread—there's no better way to work out life's little frustrations and with such yummy results!

```
3-1/4 cups all-purpose floor
    2 packages (1/4 ounce each) active dry yeast
1-1/2 cups buttermilk
  3/4 cup butter or margarine
  1/2 cup sugar
  1/2 teaspoon salt
    5 eggs
3-1/2 to 4 cups whole wheat flour, divided
    2 cups (8 ounces) shredded cheddar cheese
```

In a large mixing bowl, combine all-purpose flour and yeast. In a saucepan, heat buttermilk, butter, sugar and salt to 120°-130°; add to flour mixture. Blend on low speed until moistened. Add eggs; beat on low for 30 seconds. Beat on high for 3 minutes. Stir in enough whole wheat flour to make a soft dough.

Turn onto a floured surface; knead until smooth and elastic, about 6-8 minutes. Place in a greased bowl, turning once to grease top. Cover and let rise in a warm place until nearly doubled, about 1 hour.

Punch dough down; divide in half. On a lightly floured surface, roll each into a 12-in. x 9-in. rectangle. Cut each into three 12-in. x 3-in. strips. Combine cheese with 2 tablespoons of the remaining whole wheat flour; sprinkle 1/3 cup down center of each strip. Bring long edges together over cheese and pinch to seal. Place three strips seam side down on greased baking sheets. Braid strips together; secure ends.

Cover and let rise until doubled, about 45 minutes. Bake at 375° for 20-25 minutes or until golden. Immediately remove from baking sheets to wire racks; cool. **Yield:** 2 loaves.

Accordion Rye Rolls

Alyson Armstrong, Parkersburg, West Virginia

These rolls will make anyone like rye bread. Even though Mom fixes the dough a day ahead, she bakes them right before serving so they're hot and fresh.

```
    2 packages (1/4 ounce each) active dry yeast
  1/2 cup warm water (110° to 115°)
1-1/2 cups warm milk (110° to 115°)
  1/4 cup molasses
    4 tablespoons butter or margarine, softened,
      divided
    1 tablespoon sugar
    1 tablespoon plus 1/2 teaspoon salt, divided
    3 to 3-1/2 cups all-purpose flour
2-1/2 cups rye flour
Vegetable oil
    1 egg white
    2 teaspoons caraway seeds
```

In a mixing bowl, dissolve yeast in water. Add milk, molasses, 2 tablespoons butter, sugar and 1 tablespoon salt. Add 2 cups all-purpose flour; beat until smooth. Add rye flour and enough remaining all-purpose flour to form a soft dough.

Turn onto a floured surface; knead until smooth and elastic, about 6-8 minutes. Place in a greased bowl, turning once to grease top. Let stand for 20 minutes.

Divide dough into four portions. On a lightly floured surface, roll each portion into a 14-in. x 6-in. rectangle. Brush with remaining butter. With the blunt edge of a knife, make creases in dough at 2-in. intervals, beginning at a short side. Fold dough accordion-style back and forth along creased lines. Cut folded dough into 1-in. pieces. Place each piece cut side down in a greased muffin cup. Brush with oil. Cover loosely with plastic wrap. Refrigerate for 4-24 hours.

When ready to bake, uncover and let stand at room temperature for 10 minutes. In a small mixing bowl, beat egg white until stiff peaks form; brush over dough. Sprinkle with caraway seeds and remaining salt. Bake at 375° for 20-25 minutes or until lightly browned. **Yield:** 2 dozen.

Easy Potato Rolls

(Pictured below)

Jeanette McKinney, Belleview, Missouri

After I discovered this recipe, it became a mainstay for me. I make the dough ahead of time when company is coming, and I try to keep some in the refrigerator to make for "hay hands" on our cattle ranch. Leftover mashed potatoes are almost sure to go into these rolls.

2/3 cup shortening
2/3 cup sugar
1 cup mashed potatoes
2-1/2 teaspoons salt
2 eggs
2 packages (1/4 ounce *each*) active dry yeast
1-1/3 cups warm water (110° to 115°), *divided*
6 to 6-1/2 cups all-purpose flour

In a large mixing bowl, cream shortening and sugar. Add potatoes, salt and eggs. In a small bowl, dissolve yeast in 2/3 cup of warm water; add to creamed mixture. Beat in 2 cups flour and remaining water. Add enough remaining flour to form a soft dough. Shape into a ball; do not knead. Place in a greased bowl, turning once to grease top. Cover and let rise in a warm place until doubled, about 1 hour.

Punch dough down; divide into thirds. Shape each portion into 15 balls and arrange in three greased 9-in. round baking pans. Cover and let rise until doubled, about 30 minutes. Bake at 375° for 20-25 minutes. Remove from pans to cool on wire racks. **Yield:** 45 rolls.

Grandma's Orange Rolls

(Pictured above)

Norma Poole, Auburndale, Florida

We have our own orange trees, and it's such a pleasure to go out and pick fruit right off the tree for this yummy, yeast roll recipe.

1 package (1/4 ounce) active dry yeast
1/4 cup warm water (110° to 115°)
1 cup warm milk (110° to 115°)
1/4 cup shortening
1/4 cup sugar
1 teaspoon salt
1 egg, lightly beaten
3-1/2 to 3-3/4 cups all-purpose flour
FILLING:
1 cup sugar
1/2 cup butter *or* margarine, softened
2 tablespoons grated orange peel
GLAZE:
1 cup confectioners' sugar
4 teaspoons butter *or* margarine, softened
4 to 5 teaspoons milk
1/2 teaspoon lemon extract

In a small bowl, dissolve yeast in water. In a large mixing bowl, mix milk, shortening, sugar, salt and egg. Add yeast mixture and blend. Stir in enough flour to form a soft dough.

Turn onto a lightly floured surface; knead until smooth and elastic, about 6-8 minutes. Place in a greased bowl, turning once to grease top. Cover and let rise in a warm place until doubled, about 1 hour.

Punch dough down; divide in half. Roll each half into a 15-in. x 10-in. rectangle. Mix filling ingredients until smooth. Spread half the filling on each rectangle. Roll up, jelly-roll style, starting with a long end. Cut each into 15 rolls.

Place in two greased 11-in. x 7-in. x 2-in. baking pans. Cover and let rise until doubled, about 45 minutes. Bake at 375° for 20-25 minutes or until lightly browned. Mix glaze ingredients; spread over warm rolls. **Yield:** 30 rolls.

Whole Wheat Braids

(Pictured below)

Suella Miller, LaGrange, Indiana

There's nothing like fresh bread to complete a meal. Braiding the dough makes a pretty presentation.

 Uses less fat, sugar or salt. Includes Nutritional Analysis and Diabetic Exchanges.

- **3 packages (1/4 ounce *each*) active dry yeast**
- **3 cups warm water (110° to 115°)**
- **1/2 cup sugar**
- **3 eggs**
- **1/3 cup vegetable oil**
- **1 tablespoon salt**
- **5 cups whole wheat flour**
- **4 to 4-1/2 cups all-purpose flour**

In a mixing bowl, dissolve yeast in warm water. Add sugar, eggs, oil, salt and whole wheat flour; beat until smooth. Add enough all-purpose flour to form a soft dough.

Turn onto a floured surface; knead until smooth and elastic, about 6-8 minutes. Place in a greased bowl, turning once to grease top. Cover and let rise in a warm place until doubled, about 1 hour.

Punch dough down. Divide into nine pieces; shape each piece into a 14-in. rope and braid three ropes together. Place in three greased 8-in. x 4-in. x 2-in. loaf pans. Cover and let rise until doubled, about 30 minutes. Bake at 350° for 40-45 minutes. Remove from pans to cool on wire racks. **Yield:** 3 loaves (16 slices each).

Nutritional Analysis: One slice equals 112 calories, 138 mg sodium, 13 mg cholesterol, 20 gm carbohydrate, 3 gm protein, 2 gm fat. **Diabetic Exchange:** 1-1/2 starch.

Strawberries 'n' Cream Bread

Suzanne Randall, Dexter, Maine

Once strawberry-picking time arrives here each summer, my husband and I look forward to this bread. Since only fresh strawberries will work well in the recipe, I have been thinking of trying a different kind of berry...so we can enjoy it more often.

- **1/2 cup butter *or* margarine, softened**
- **3/4 cup sugar**
- **2 eggs**
- **1/2 cup sour cream**
- **1 teaspoon vanilla extract**
- **1-3/4 cups all-purpose flour**
- **1/2 teaspoon baking powder**
- **1/2 teaspoon baking soda**
- **1/2 teaspoon salt**
- **1/4 teaspoon ground cinnamon**
- **3/4 cup chopped fresh strawberries**
- **3/4 cup chopped walnuts, toasted, *divided***

In a mixing bowl, cream butter and sugar until fluffy. Beat in eggs, one at a time, beating well after each addition. Add sour cream and vanilla; mix well. Combine the flour, baking powder, baking soda, salt and cinnamon; stir into creamed mixture just until moistened. Fold in strawberries and 1/2 cup nuts.

Pour into a greased 8-in. x 4-in. x 2-in. loaf pan. Sprinkle with remaining nuts. Bake at 350° for 65-70 minutes or until a toothpick inserted near the center comes out clean. Cool for 10 minutes; remove from pan to a wire rack to cool completely. **Yield:** 1 loaf.

Milk-and-Honey White Bread

Kathy McCreary, Goddard, Kansas

My dad has been a wheat farmer all his life and my state is the wheat capital, so this recipe represents my region and my family well. This bread never lasts too long at our house. My family gobbles it up as fast as I can bake loaves of it.

- **1 package (1/4 ounce) active dry yeast**
- **2-1/2 cups warm milk (110° to 115°)**
- **1/3 cup honey**
- **1/4 cup butter *or* margarine, melted**
- **2 teaspoons salt**
- **8 to 8-1/2 cups all-purpose flour**

In a mixing bowl, dissolve yeast in warm milk. Add honey, butter, salt and 5 cups of flour; beat until smooth. Add enough remaining flour to form a soft dough.

Turn onto a floured surface; knead until smooth and elastic, about 6-8 minutes. Place in a greased bowl, turning once to grease top. Cover and let rise in a warm place until doubled, about 1 hour.

Punch dough down and shape into two loaves. Place in greased 9-in. x 5-in. x 3-in. loaf pans. Cover and let rise until doubled, about 30 minutes. Bake at 375° for 30-35 minutes or until golden brown. Cover with foil if necessary to prevent overbrowning. Remove from pans and cool on wire racks. **Yield:** 2 loaves.

Feather-Light Biscuits

(Pictured at right)

Eleanore Hill, Fresno, California

I usually use a glass or baking powder can lid as a cutter so my biscuits will be bigger than average size...and I always bake some extras to send home with the kids.

> 6 cups biscuit/baking mix
> 1/4 cup sugar
> 1 package (1/4 ounce) active dry yeast
> 1/3 cup shortening
> 1 to 1-1/4 cups warm water (120° to 130°)
> 1/4 cup butter or margarine, melted

In a large bowl, combine the biscuit mix, sugar and yeast. Cut in shortening until mixture resembles coarse crumbs. Stir in enough warm water to make a soft and slightly sticky dough.

Turn onto a floured surface; knead gently 3-4 times. Roll dough to 3/4-in. thickness; cut with a 2-1/2-in. round biscuit cutter. Place on ungreased baking sheets. Brush tops with melted butter. Bake at 400° for 10-12 minutes or until lightly browned. **Yield:** about 2 dozen.

Pumpkin Spice Bread

(Pictured below)

Delora Lucas, Belle, West Virginia

This recipe is at least 40 years old and makes a very moist bread. It's been described as tasting like pumpkin pie without the crust.

> 3 cups sugar
> 1 cup vegetable oil
> 4 eggs, lightly beaten
> 1 can (16 ounces) solid-pack pumpkin
> 3-1/2 cups all-purpose flour
> 2 teaspoons baking soda
> 1 teaspoon baking powder
> 1 teaspoon salt
> 1 teaspoon ground cinnamon
> 1 teaspoon ground nutmeg
> 1/2 teaspoon ground cloves
> 1/2 teaspoon ground allspice
> 1/2 cup water

In a large bowl, combine sugar, oil and eggs. Add pumpkin and mix well. Combine dry ingredients; add to the pumpkin mixture alternately with water. Pour into two greased 9-in. x 5-in. x 3-in. loaf pans. Bake at 350° for 60-70 minutes or until bread tests done. Cool in pans 10 minutes before removing to a wire rack; cool completely. **Yield:** 2 loaves.

Bread 'n' Butter

FOR special occasions, serve butter for your homemade bread in fun ways:
- To create butter cutouts, slice a chilled stick of butter 1/4 inch thick. Cut out shapes with small cookie cutters.
- To make balls of butter, cut balls from a chilled 1-pound block of butter using a large melon baller dipped in hot water.
- Arrange butter cutouts or balls on crushed ice in a small decorative bowl.

> 1 package (1/4 ounce) active dry yeast
> 1-1/2 cups warm water (110° to 115°), *divided*
> 1 tablespoon sugar
> 2 teaspoons salt
> 1 tablespoon shortening, melted
> 4 cups all-purpose flour

Cornmeal

In a mixing bowl, dissolve yeast in 1/2 cup water. Add sugar, salt, shortening and remaining water; stir until dissolved. Add flour and stir until smooth (do not knead). Cover and let rise in a warm place for 1 hour or until doubled.

Turn onto a floured surface. Divide in half; let rest for 10 minutes. Roll each half into a 10-in. x 8-in. rectangle. Roll up from a long side; pinch to seal. Place seam side down on greased baking sheets sprinkled with cornmeal. Sprinkle the tops with cornmeal.

Cover and let rise until doubled, about 45 minutes. With a very sharp knife, make five diagonal cuts across the top of each loaf. Bake at 400° for 20-30 minutes or until lightly browned. Cool on wire racks. **Yield:** 2 loaves (10 slices each).

Nutritional Analysis: One slice equals 100 calories, 233 mg sodium, 0 cholesterol, 20 gm carbohydrate, 3 gm protein, 1 gm fat. **Diabetic Exchange:** 1-1/2 starch.

Parmesan Knots

(Pictured above)

Cathy Adams, Parkersburg, West Virginia

Use refrigerated biscuits to make a big batch of these buttery snacks. They're handy to keep in the freezer and a snap to reheat and serve with a meal.

> 1/2 cup vegetable oil
> 1/4 cup grated Parmesan cheese
> 1-1/2 teaspoons dried parsley flakes
> 1-1/2 teaspoons dried oregano
> 1 teaspoon garlic powder

Dash pepper

> 3 cans (12 ounces *each*) refrigerated buttermilk biscuits

In a small bowl, combine oil, cheese, parsley, oregano, garlic powder and pepper; set aside. Cut each biscuit in half. Roll each portion into a 6-in. rope; tie in a loose knot. Place on greased baking sheets. Bake at 450° for 6-8 minutes or until golden brown.

Immediately brush with the Parmesan mixture, then brush again. Serve warm or freeze for up to 2 months. To use frozen rolls: Bake at 350° for 6-8 minutes or until heated through. **Yield:** 5 dozen.

Crusty French Bread

Christy Freeman, Central Point, Oregon

I love to treat guests to these golden brown, crusty loaves. Don't hesitate to try this recipe even if you are not an accomplished bread baker—there's no kneading required!

Raspberry Coffee Cake

Marian Cummings, West Paris, Maine

I developed this recipe to share our raspberry bounty with guests. The pretty crumb-topped cake's fruity flavor really shines through.

> 1 cup plus 3 tablespoons sugar, *divided*
> 1/4 cup cornstarch
> 3 cups fresh *or* frozen unsweetened raspberries
> 2 cups biscuit/baking mix
> 2/3 cup milk
> 2 eggs
> 2 tablespoons vegetable oil

TOPPING:

> 1 package (3.4 ounces) instant vanilla pudding mix

Shaping Rolls

INSTEAD of just making a traditional round dinner roll, try one of these techniques:

- For knot-shaped rolls, shape dough into 3-inch balls. Roll each ball into a rope. Tie a knot; tuck and pinch ends.
- For crescent rolls, roll a portion of dough into a 12-inch circle. Cut into wedges. Roll up from the wide end.
- For cloverleaf rolls, shape dough into 1-1/2-inch balls. Place three balls in each greased muffin cup.

ture just until moistened. Fold in blueberries (batter will be thick). Fill greased or paper-lined miniature muffin cups with about a tablespoon of batter. Sprinkle with sugar if desired. Bake at 400° for 10-15 minutes or until muffins test done. Cool for 5 minutes before removing from pan to a wire rack. **Yield:** 7 dozen.

Cinnamon Crescents

(Pictured below)

Emily Engel, Quill Lake, Saskatchewan

I've had the recipe for these crispy cinnamon-sugar roll-ups for years. They're one of my family's favorites and so easy to make. We enjoy them at breakfast with a cup of coffee.

> 2-1/2 cups all-purpose flour
> 1 teaspoon baking powder
> 1 cup cold butter *or* margarine
> 1/2 cup milk
> 1 egg, beaten
> 1 cup sugar
> 4 teaspoons ground cinnamon

Combine flour and baking powder in a large bowl; cut in butter until crumbly. Stir in milk and egg. Divide into three portions; shape each portion into a ball. Combine sugar and cinnamon; sprinkle a third over a pastry board or a surface.

Roll one ball into a 12-in. circle; cut into 12 wedges. Roll up from wide edge. Repeat with the remaining dough and cinnamon-sugar. Place rolls with point side down on lightly greased baking sheets; form into crescent shapes. Bake at 350° for 16-18 minutes or until lightly browned (do not overbake). **Yield:** 3 dozen.

> 1/2 cup sugar
> 1/4 cup cold butter *or* margarine

In a saucepan, combine 1 cup of sugar and cornstarch. Add raspberries; bring to a boil over medium heat. Boil for 2 minutes, stirring constantly. Remove from the heat; allow to cool.

Meanwhile, in a mixing bowl, combine the biscuit mix, milk, eggs, oil and remaining sugar; mix well. Spread two-thirds of the batter into a greased 13-in. x 9-in. x 2-in. baking pan. Spread with raspberry mixture. Spoon remaining batter over top. For topping, combine pudding mix and sugar. Cut in butter until crumbly; sprinkle over batter. Bake at 350° for 35-40 minutes. **Yield:** 12 servings.

Blueberry Mini Muffins

(Pictured above)

Suzanne Fredette, Littleton, Massachusetts

These bite-size muffins are popular in our family. Plus, they're especially nice for potlucks.

> 1 cup butter *or* margarine, softened
> 2 cups sugar
> 5 eggs
> 1 cup buttermilk
> 2 teaspoons vanilla extract
> 5 cups all-purpose flour
> 1 teaspoon baking soda
> 1 teaspoon baking powder
> 3/4 teaspoon salt
> 3 cups fresh *or* frozen blueberries
> Additional sugar, optional

In a mixing bowl, cream butter and sugar. Add eggs, buttermilk and vanilla; mix well. Combine flour, baking soda, baking powder and salt; stir into the creamed mix-

Sweet Treats

Old-Fashioned
Whoopie Pies (p. 81)

Chapter 7

Best Cake Brownies

(Pictured below)

Jean Kennedy, Springfield, Oregon

This recipe caught my eye because it uses a whole can of chocolate syrup! I had searched for years for a brownie everyone likes, and this is it. My husband takes them to work, and they're gone in no time. They cut nicely after cooling a bit.

        1/2 cup butter *or* margarine, softened
          1 cup sugar
          4 eggs
          1 can (16 ounces) chocolate syrup
          1 teaspoon vanilla extract
          1 cup all-purpose flour
        1/2 teaspoon salt
GLAZE:
          1 cup sugar
        1/3 cup butter *or* margarine
        1/3 cup milk
        2/3 cup semisweet chocolate chips
        2/3 cup miniature marshmallows

In a mixing bowl, cream butter and sugar. Add the eggs, one at a time, beating well after each addition. Beat in chocolate syrup and vanilla. Add the flour and salt until blended. Pour into a greased 15-in. x 10-in. x 1-in. baking pan. Bake at 350° for 20-25 minutes or until a toothpick inserted near the center comes out clean (top of brownies will still appear wet). Cool on a wire rack for 15-20 minutes.

Meanwhile, in a small saucepan, combine sugar, butter and milk. Bring to a boil; boil until the sugar is dissolved. Remove from the heat; stir in chocolate chips and marshmallows until melted. Pour over the brownies and spread evenly. Refrigerate for 5 minutes before cutting. **Yield:** about 3 dozen.

Toffee Almond Sandies

(Pictured above)

Alice Kahnk, Kennard, Nebraska

Crisp and loaded with goodies, these are my husband's favorite cookies. I used to bake them in large batches when our four sons still lived at home. Now I whip them up for our grandchildren.

          1 cup butter (no substitutes), softened
          1 cup sugar
          1 cup confectioners' sugar
          1 cup vegetable oil
          2 eggs
          1 teaspoon almond extract
      3-1/2 cups all-purpose flour
          1 cup whole wheat flour
          1 teaspoon baking soda
          1 teaspoon cream of tartar
          1 teaspoon salt
          2 cups chopped almonds
          1 package (6 ounces) English toffee bits
Additional sugar

In a mixing bowl, cream butter and sugars. Add oil, eggs and extract; mix well. Combine flours, baking soda, cream of tartar and salt; gradually add to creamed mixture. Stir in almonds and toffee bits. Shape into 1-in. balls; roll in sugar. Place on ungreased baking sheets and flatten with a fork. Bake at 350° for 12-14 minutes or until lightly browned. **Yield:** about 12 dozen.

Cinnamon Crackle Cookies

Vicki Lair, Apple Valley, Minnesota

This recipe is the compilation of many years of baking. I make these cookies for a holiday bazaar and year-round for our family. They freeze well.

1/2 cup butter (no substitutes), softened
1/2 cup shortening
1 cup sugar
1/2 cup packed brown sugar
1 egg
1 teaspoon vanilla extract
1/2 teaspoon almond extract
2-1/2 cups all-purpose flour
1 tablespoon ground cinnamon
2 teaspoons baking soda
2 teaspoons cream of tartar
2 teaspoons ground nutmeg
2 teaspoons grated orange peel
1 teaspoon grated lemon peel
1/2 teaspoon salt
Additional sugar

In a mixing bowl, cream butter, shortening and sugars. Add egg and extracts; mix well. Combine the next eight ingredients; gradually add to the creamed mixture. Shape into 1-in. balls; roll in sugar. Place 2 in. apart on ungreased baking sheets. Bake at 350° for 10-15 minutes or until lightly browned. **Yield:** about 6 dozen.

Peanut Butter Chocolate Chip Cookies

Clarice Schweitzer, Sun City, Arizona

Here's a different version of the traditional favorite chocolate chip cookie that I think is especially good.

1/2 cup butter *or* margarine, softened
1/2 cup sugar
1/3 cup packed brown sugar
1/2 cup chunky peanut butter
1 egg
1 teaspoon vanilla extract
1 cup all-purpose flour
1/2 cup old-fashioned oats
1 teaspoon baking soda
1/4 teaspoon salt
1 cup (6 ounces) semisweet chocolate chips

In a mixing bowl, cream butter and sugars; beat in peanut butter, egg and vanilla. Combine flour, oats, baking soda and salt; stir into the creamed mixture. Stir in chocolate chips. Drop by rounded tablespoonfuls onto ungreased baking sheets. Bake at 350° for 10-12 minutes or until golden brown. Cool 1 minute before removing to a wire rack. **Yield:** 2 dozen.

Cherry Cheese Pizza

(Pictured at right)

Elaine Darbyshire, Golden, British Columbia

This dessert pizza is a great way to use cherries—my family likes it better than cherry pie. Each bite just melts in your mouth. People who sample it rave about this "sweet" pizza—when my neighbor tried a piece, she couldn't stop saying "Mmm..." the entire time.

1 cup all-purpose flour
1/8 teaspoon baking powder
1/4 cup cold butter *or* margarine
2 tablespoons shortening
3 to 4 tablespoons water
1 package (8 ounces) cream cheese, softened
1/2 cup sugar
2 eggs
1 teaspoon vanilla extract
1/3 cup chopped pecans *or* almonds
TOPPING:
2-1/2 cups fresh *or* frozen pitted tart cherries *or* 1 can (15 ounces) tart cherries
1/3 cup sugar
2 tablespoons cornstarch
1 tablespoon butter *or* margarine
1/8 teaspoon almond extract
1/8 teaspoon red food coloring
Whipped cream and fresh mint, optional

In a bowl, combine flour and baking powder; cut in butter and shortening until mixture resembles coarse crumbs. Gradually add water, tossing with a fork until dough forms a ball. Roll out into a 14-in. circle. Place on an ungreased 12-in. pizza pan. Flute edges to form a rim; prick bottom of crust. Bake at 350° for 15 minutes.

In a mixing bowl, beat cream cheese and sugar until smooth. Beat in eggs and vanilla. Stir in nuts. Spread over crust. Bake 10 minutes longer. Cool. Drain cherries, reserving 1/3 cup juice. Set cherries and juice aside. In a saucepan, combine sugar and cornstarch; stir in reserved juice until smooth. Add cherries. Cook and stir over medium heat until mixture comes to a boil. Cook and stir 2 minutes longer. Remove from the heat; stir in butter, extract and food coloring. Cool to room temperature; spread over cream cheese layer. Garnish with whipped cream and mint if desired. **Yield:** 10-12 slices.

Fluffy Pineapple Torte

(Pictured below)

Gina Squires, Salem, Oregon

This fluffy dessert is so good after a hearty meal because even a big slice is as light as a feather.

1-1/2 cups graham cracker crumbs
1/4 cup butter *or* margarine, melted
2 tablespoons sugar
FILLING:
1 can (12 ounces) evaporated milk
1 package (3 ounces) lemon gelatin
1 cup boiling water
1 package (8 ounces) cream cheese, softened
1/2 cup sugar
1 can (8 ounces) crushed pineapple, drained
1 cup chopped walnuts, *divided*

Combine crumbs, butter and sugar; press into the bottom of a 13-in. x 9-in. x 2-in. baking pan. Bake at 325° for 10 minutes; cool. Pour evaporated milk into a metal mixing bowl. Add the mixer beaters. Cover and chill bowl and beaters for at least 2 hours. Meanwhile, dissolve gelatin in water; chill until syrupy, about 30 minutes.

Remove milk from refrigerator and beat until stiff peaks form. In a large mixing bowl, beat cream cheese and sugar until smooth. Add gelatin; mix well. Stir in pineapple and 3/4 cup walnuts. Fold in milk. Pour over crust. Chill for at least 3 hours or overnight. Sprinkle remaining walnuts over the top before filling is completely firm. **Yield:** 12 servings.

Cream-Filled Cupcakes

(Pictured above right)

Edie DeSpain, Logan, Utah

Folks who enjoy homemade chocolate cupcakes are even more impressed when they bite into these treats

and find a fluffy cream filling. These are great in a lunch box or on a buffet table.

3 cups all-purpose flour
2 cups sugar
1/3 cup baking cocoa
2 teaspoons baking soda
1 teaspoon salt
2 eggs
1 cup milk
1 cup vegetable oil
1 cup water
1 teaspoon vanilla extract
FILLING:
1/4 cup butter *or* margarine, softened
1/4 cup shortening
2 cups confectioners' sugar
3 tablespoons milk
1 teaspoon vanilla extract
Pinch salt
Chocolate frosting

In a mixing bowl, combine the first five ingredients. Add eggs, milk, oil, water and vanilla. Beat until smooth, about 2 minutes. Fill paper-lined muffin cups half full. Bake at 375° for 15-20 minutes or until a toothpick inserted near the center comes out clean. Remove from pans to wire racks to cool completely.

In a mixing bowl, combine butter, shortening, confectioners' sugar, milk, vanilla and salt; beat until fluffy, about 5 minutes. Insert a very small tip into a pastry or plastic bag; fill with cream filling. Push the tip through the bottom of paper liner to fill each cupcake. Frost tops with chocolate frosting. **Yield:** 3 dozen.

Chocolate Caramel Bars

Betty Hagerty, Philadelphia, Pennsylvania

These rich, gooey bars are my most-requested treats. They're popular at school functions, family barbecues and picnics.

2-1/4 cups all-purpose flour, *divided*
   2 cups quick-cooking oats
1-1/2 cups packed brown sugar
   1 teaspoon baking soda
  1/2 teaspoon salt
1-1/2 cups cold butter *or* margarine
   2 cups (12 ounces) semisweet chocolate chips
   1 cup chopped pecans
   1 jar (12 ounces) caramel ice cream topping

In a bowl, combine 2 cups flour, oats, brown sugar, baking soda and salt. Cut in butter until crumbly. Set half aside for topping. Press the remaining crumb mixture into a greased 13-in. x 9-in. x 2-in. baking pan. Bake at 350° for 15 minutes.

Sprinkle with the chocolate chips and pecans. Whisk caramel topping and remaining flour until smooth; drizzle over top. Sprinkle with the reserved crumb mixture. Bake for 18-20 minutes or until golden brown. Cool on a wire rack for 2 hours before cutting. **Yield:** about 4-1/2 dozen.

Caramel Apple Cake

Paulette Reyenga, Brantford, Ontario

A wonderful harvest of apples that we picked up at a local orchard one year inspired me to adjust a recipe I'd seen and come up with this moist cake. After we were married, I learned through trial and error (at times, lots of those!) to cook for my husband.

  1/2 cup chopped walnuts
  1/3 cup packed brown sugar
   1 cup flaked coconut
2-1/2 cups all-purpose flour
1-1/2 cups sugar
1-1/2 teaspoons baking soda
   1 teaspoon salt
  1/2 cup baking powder
  1/4 teaspoon ground cinnamon
   2 eggs
  1/2 cup evaporated milk
  1/3 cup water
   2 cups finely shredded peeled apples
CARAMEL TOPPING:
  1/3 cup packed brown sugar
  1/4 cup evaporated milk
   2 tablespoons butter *or* margarine

Combine walnuts, brown sugar and coconut; set aside. In a mixing bowl, combine the next six ingredients. In a small bowl, combine eggs, milk, water and apples; add to flour mixture. Mix well. Pour into a greased 13-in. x 9-in. x 2-in. baking pan. Sprinkle with nut mixture. Bake at 325° for 45-50 minutes or until a toothpick inserted near the center comes out clean.

Meanwhile, in a heavy saucepan, combine the topping ingredients; cook over medium heat, stirring constantly, until the sugar is dissolved and the mixture has thickened slightly, about 8 minutes. Poke holes with a fork in top of the hot cake; immediately spoon topping over cake. Cool completely on a wire rack. **Yield:** 12-15 servings.

Old-Fashioned Whoopie Pies

(Pictured above)

Maria Costello, Monroe, North Carolina

Who can resist soft chocolate sandwich cookies filled with a layer of fluffy white frosting? Mom has made these for years...they're a treat that never lasted very long with me and my two brothers around.

  1/2 cup baking cocoa
  1/2 cup hot water
  1/2 cup shortening
1-1/2 cups sugar
   2 eggs
   1 teaspoon vanilla extract
2-2/3 cups all-purpose flour
   1 teaspoon baking powder
   1 teaspoon baking soda
  1/4 teaspoon salt
  1/2 cup buttermilk
FILLING:
   3 tablespoons all-purpose flour
Dash salt
   1 cup milk
  3/4 cup shortening
1-1/2 cups confectioners' sugar
   2 teaspoons vanilla extract

In a small bowl, combine cocoa and water; mix well. Cool for 5 minutes. In a mixing bowl, cream shortening and sugar. Add cocoa mixture, eggs and vanilla; mix well. Combine dry ingredients. Add to creamed mixture alternately with buttermilk; mix well. Drop by rounded tablespoonfuls 2 in. apart onto greased baking sheets. Flatten slightly with a spoon. Bake at 350° for 10-12 minutes or until firm to the touch. Remove to wire racks.

In a saucepan, combine flour and salt. Gradually whisk in milk until smooth; cook and stir over medium-high heat until thick, about 5-7 minutes. Remove from heat. Cover and refrigerate until completely cool. In a mixing bowl, cream shortening, sugar and vanilla. Add chilled milk mixture; beat for 7 minutes or until fluffy. Spread filling on half of the cookies; top with remaining cookies. Store in the refrigerator. **Yield:** 2 dozen.

Streusel Pumpkin Pie

Bertha Johnson, Indianapolis, Indiana

Basic pumpkin pie is good, but we think this dressed-up version is even better. Plenty of pecans add a nutty crunch to the pastry and the streusel topping. It's a perfect dessert for Thanksgiving or any time you want to end a dinner with something special.

        2 cups all-purpose flour
    1/4 cup finely chopped pecans
        1 teaspoon salt
    2/3 cup plus 1 tablespoon vegetable shortening
      4 to 5 tablespoons water
FILLING:
        1 can (30 ounces) pumpkin pie mix
        1 can (14 ounces) sweetened condensed milk
        1 egg, lightly beaten
STREUSEL TOPPING:
    1/2 cup packed brown sugar
    1/4 cup all-purpose flour
    1/4 cup chopped pecans
    1/2 teaspoon ground cinnamon
        3 tablespoons cold butter *or* margarine

In a bowl, combine flour, pecans and salt; cut in the shortening until crumbly. Gradually add water, tossing with a fork until a ball forms. Divide dough in half. Roll out each portion to fit a 9-in. pie plate; place pastry in pie plates. Flute edges and set aside. Combine pie mix, milk and egg; pour into pastry shells.

For topping, combine brown sugar, flour, pecans and cinnamon in a small bowl; cut in butter until crumbly. Sprinkle over filling. Cover edges of pastry loosely with foil. Bake at 375° for 40-45 minutes or until a knife inserted near the center comes out clean. Cool on a wire rack for 2 hours. Refrigerate until serving. **Yield:** 2 pies (6-8 servings each).

Macadamia Nut Cookies

Mary Gaylord, Balsam Lake, Wisconsin

These rich cookies—full of Hawaiian macadamia nuts and chocolate chips—are simply scrumptious.

        1 cup butter *or* margarine, softened
    3/4 cup sugar
    3/4 cup packed brown sugar
        2 eggs
        1 teaspoon vanilla extract
    2-1/4 cups all-purpose flour
        1 teaspoon baking soda
        1 teaspoon salt
        2 jars (3-1/2 ounces *each*) macadamia nuts,
            chopped
        2 cups (12 ounces) semisweet chocolate chips
        1 cup (6 ounces) vanilla baking chips

In a mixing bowl, cream butter and sugars. Add eggs and vanilla; beat on medium speed for 2 minutes. Combine flour, baking soda and salt; add to creamed mixture and beat for 2 minutes. Stir in nuts and chips. Cover and refrigerate several hours or overnight. Drop by tablespoonfuls 2 in. apart onto ungreased baking

sheets. Bake at 375° for 10-12 minutes or until golden brown. Cool on pans for 1 minute before removing to wire racks; cool completely. **Yield:** about 6 dozen.

Editor's Note: 2 cups of chopped almonds may be substituted for the macadamia nuts.

Berry Big Pie

(Pictured above)

Janelle Seward, Ontario, Oregon

I take this giant pie to almost every potluck. The crust is so easy, and we have lots of berries since they grow here on our small acreage. With a dessert this size, everyone can enjoy a luscious piece.

        4 cups all-purpose flour
        1 tablespoon sugar
        2 teaspoons salt
    1-3/4 cups cold shortening
    1/2 cup cold water
        1 egg
        1 tablespoon white vinegar
FILLING:
        8 cups fresh *or* frozen blackberries*
        2 cups sugar
    1/2 cup all-purpose flour
Half-and-half cream

In a large bowl, combine flour, sugar and salt; cut in shortening until mixture resembles coarse crumbs. In a bowl, combine water, egg and vinegar; stir into flour mixture just until moistened. Form into a roll. Cover and refrigerate for 1 hour.

On a floured surface, roll two-thirds of the dough into an 18-in. x 14-in. rectangle. Carefully place onto the bottom and up the sides of a 13-in. x 9-in. x 2-in. glass baking dish. Combine berries, sugar and flour; pour into crust. Use the remaining dough to make lattice strips; place over the filling. Brush pastry with cream. Bake at 400° for 15 minutes; reduce heat to 350°. Bake about 1 hour longer or until bubbly. Cool completely. Store in the refrigerator. **Yield:** 12-16 servings.

Editor's Note: If using frozen berries, do not thaw.

Peanut Butter Sandwich Cookies

(Pictured below)

Debbie Kokes, Tabor, South Dakota

I'm a busy mother of two young children. I work in our school office and help my husband on our hog and cattle farm. When I find time to bake a treat, I like it to be special. The creamy filling gives traditional peanut butter cookies a new twist.

    1 cup butter-flavored shortening
    1 cup creamy peanut butter
    1 cup sugar
    1 cup packed brown sugar
    1 teaspoon vanilla extract
    3 eggs
    3 cups all-purpose flour
    2 teaspoons baking soda
    1/4 teaspoon salt
FILLING:
    1/2 cup creamy peanut butter
    3 cups confectioners' sugar
    1 teaspoon vanilla extract
    5 to 6 tablespoons milk

In a mixing bowl, cream the shortening, peanut butter and sugars. Add vanilla. Add eggs, one at a time, beating well after each addition. Combine flour, baking soda and salt; add to creamed mixture. Shape into 1-in. balls and place 2 in. apart on ungreased baking sheets. Flatten to 3/8-in. thickness with a fork. Bake at 375° for

7-8 minutes or until golden. Cool on wire racks. In a mixing bowl, beat filling ingredients until smooth. Spread on half of the cookies and top each with another cookie. **Yield:** about 4 dozen.

Lemon Butter Cookies

(Pictured above)

Judy McCreight, Springfield, Illinois

These tender cutout cookies have a slight lemon flavor that makes them stand out from the rest. They're very easy to roll out compared to other sugar cookies I've worked with. I know you'll enjoy them as much as my family does.

    1 cup butter (no substitutes), softened
    2 cups sugar
    2 eggs, beaten
    1/4 cup milk
    2 teaspoons lemon extract
    1/2 teaspoon salt
4-1/2 cups all-purpose flour
    2 teaspoons baking powder
    1/4 teaspoon baking soda
Colored sugar, optional

In a mixing bowl, cream butter and sugar. Add eggs, milk and extract. Combine dry ingredients; gradually add to creamed mixture. Cover and chill for 2 hours. Roll out on a lightly floured surface to 1/8-in. thickness. Cut with a 2-in. cookie cutter dipped in flour. Place 2 in. apart on ungreased baking sheets. Sprinkle with colored sugar if desired. Bake at 350° for 8-9 minutes or until the edges just begin to brown. Remove to wire racks to cool. **Yield:** about 13 dozen.

Fruit 'n' Nut Cookies

Jennie Loftus, Gasport, New York

Once after making a fruitcake, I had some fruit and nuts left over. I mixed them into a basic cookie dough along with pineapple and coconut. The result was these soft, colorful cookies, which are a nice addition to a Christmas dessert tray.

    3/4 cup butter *or* margarine, softened
    3/4 cup shortening
1-1/4 cups packed brown sugar
      2 eggs
      1 teaspoon vanilla extract
      4 cups all-purpose flour
      2 teaspoons baking powder
    1/2 teaspoon salt
      1 can (8 ounces) crushed pineapple, drained
    1/2 cup chopped dates
    1/2 cup chopped red maraschino cherries
    1/2 cup chopped green maraschino cherries
    1/2 cup flaked coconut
    1/2 cup chopped pecans *or* walnuts

In a large mixing bowl, cream the butter, shortening and brown sugar. Add eggs, one at a time, beating well after each addition. Beat in vanilla. Combine flour, baking powder and salt; gradually add to the creamed mixture. Stir in remaining ingredients.

Shape into three 10-in. rolls; wrap each roll in plastic wrap. Refrigerate for 2 hours or until firm. Unwrap and cut into 1/4-in. slices. Place 2 in. apart on ungreased baking sheets. Bake at 375° for 8-10 minutes or until golden brown. Remove to wire racks to cool. **Yield:** 7 dozen.

Upside-Down Strawberry Shortcake

(Pictured above)

Debra Falkiner, St. Charles, Missouri

For a tasty twist at dessert time, this special dessert has a bountiful berry layer on the bottom. The tempting cake is a treat our family has savored for years.

      1 cup miniature marshmallows
      1 package (16 ounces) frozen sweetened sliced strawberries, thawed
      1 package (3 ounces) strawberry gelatin
    1/2 cup shortening
1-1/2 cups sugar
      3 eggs
      1 teaspoon vanilla extract
2-1/4 cups all-purpose flour
      3 teaspoons baking powder
    1/2 teaspoon salt
      1 cup milk
Fresh strawberries and whipped cream

Sprinkle marshmallows evenly into a greased 13-in. x 9-in. x 2-in. baking dish; set aside. In a bowl, combine strawberries and gelatin powder; set aside. In a mixing bowl, cream shortening and sugar. Add the eggs, one at a time, beating well after each addition. Beat in vanilla. Combine flour, baking powder and salt; add to creamed mixture alternately with milk.

Pour batter over the marshmallows. Spoon strawberry mixture evenly over batter. Bake at 350° for 45-50 minutes or until a toothpick inserted near the center comes out clean. Cool on a wire rack. Cut into squares. Garnish with strawberries and whipped cream. **Yield:** 12-16 servings.

Marshmallow Graham Dessert

Lucile Proctor, Panguitch, Utah

My siblings and I could always find room for one of these cool, yummy dessert squares even after a very filling meal. For a light and fluffy treat, this sweet and creamy blend with bits of pineapple mixed in just can't be beat!

      1 package (16 ounces) large marshmallows
      2 cups milk
1-1/2 teaspoons lemon extract
      1 can (20 ounces) crushed pineapple, drained
      2 cups whipping cream, whipped
      2 cups graham cracker crumbs (about 32 squares)
    1/2 cup butter *or* margarine, melted

In a heavy saucepan over low heat, melt marshmallows and milk. Remove from the heat. Cool, stirring occasionally. Stir in extract. Fold in pineapple and whipped cream. Combine cracker crumbs and butter. Press 1-1/2 cups into a greased 13-in. x 9-in. x 2-in. pan. Spread with the pineapple mixture. Sprinkle with the remaining crumb mixture. Refrigerate for 2-3 hours before serving. **Yield:** 12-16 servings.

Shortbread Lemon Bars

(Pictured above)

Margaret Peterson, Forest City, Iowa

I've put together two family cookbooks over the years, and this recipe ranks among my favorites. These special lemon bars have a yummy shortbread crust and a refreshing flavor.

1-1/2 cups all-purpose flour
 1/2 cup confectioners' sugar
  1 teaspoon grated lemon peel
  1 teaspoon grated orange peel
 3/4 cup cold butter *or* margarine
FILLING:
  4 eggs
  2 cups sugar
 1/3 cup lemon juice
 1/4 cup all-purpose flour
  2 teaspoons grated lemon peel
  2 teaspoons grated orange peel
  1 teaspoon baking powder
TOPPING:
  2 cups (16 ounces) sour cream
 1/3 cup sugar
 1/2 teaspoon vanilla extract

In a food processor, combine flour, confectioners' sugar, and lemon and orange peel. Cut in butter until crumbly; process until mixture forms a ball. Pat into a greased 13-in. x 9-in. x 2-in. baking pan. Bake at 350° for 12-14 minutes or until set and the edges are lightly browned.

Meanwhile, in a mixing bowl, combine the filling ingredients; mix well. Pour over hot crust. Bake for 14-16 minutes or until set and lightly browned.

Meanwhile, in a bowl, combine topping ingredients. Spread over filling. Bake 7-9 minutes longer or until topping is set. Cool on a wire rack. Refrigerate overnight. Cut into bars just before serving. **Yield:** 3 dozen.

Tangy Lemon Cheesecake

(Pictured below)

Pam Persons, Towanda, Kansas

This dessert gets added spark from a gingersnap crust and a luscious lemon sauce. The mix of sweet and tart is unexpected and delightful. I came up with the recipe based on several others I encountered on a trip to California with my husband for our 15th anniversary.

2-1/2 cups crushed gingersnaps (about 40 cookies)
 1/3 cup butter *or* margarine, melted
FILLING:
  **3 packages (8 ounces *each*) cream cheese,
    softened**
  1 cup sugar
  3 eggs
  1 tablespoon lemon juice
  1 tablespoon vanilla extract
SAUCE:
 1/2 cup sugar
  2 tablespoons cornstarch
 3/4 cup water
  2 tablespoons butter *or* margarine
 1/4 cup lemon juice
  1 tablespoon grated lemon peel

In a small bowl, combine cookie crumbs and butter; mix well. Press onto the bottom and 2 in. up the sides of a greased 9-in. springform pan; set aside. In a mixing bowl, beat cream cheese and sugar until smooth. Add eggs; beat on low just until combined. Add lemon juice and vanilla; beat just until blended. Pour into crust. Bake at 350° for 35-40 minutes or until center is almost set. Cool on a wire rack for 10 minutes. Carefully run a knife around the edge of pan to loosen; cool 1 hour longer.

In a saucepan, combine sugar and cornstarch. Stir in water until smooth; bring to a boil. Reduce heat; cook and stir over medium heat for 2 minutes or until thickened. Remove from heat; stir in butter, lemon juice and peel. Refrigerate cheesecake and sauce overnight. Serve sauce over cheesecake. **Yield:** 12 servings.

Butterscotch Pecan Dessert

(Pictured above)

Becky Harrison, Albion, Illinois

Light and creamy, this terrific treat never lasts long when I serve it to family and friends. The fluffy cream cheese layer topped with cool butterscotch pudding is a lip-smacking combination. It's also pretty when put out on a potluck table.

- 1/2 cup cold butter *or* margarine
- 1 cup all-purpose flour
- 3/4 cup chopped pecans, *divided*
- 1 package (8 ounces) cream cheese, softened
- 1 cup confectioners' sugar
- 1 carton (8 ounces) frozen whipped topping, thawed, *divided*
- 3-1/2 cups milk
- 2 packages (3.4 *or* 3.5 ounces *each*) instant butterscotch *or* vanilla pudding mix

In a bowl, cut the butter into the flour until crumbly; stir in 1/2 cup pecans. Press into an ungreased 13-in. x 9-in. x 2-in. baking pan. Bake at 350° for 20 minutes or until lightly browned. Cool.

In a mixing bowl, beat cream cheese and sugar until fluffy. Fold in 1 cup whipped topping; spread over crust. Combine milk and pudding mix until smooth; pour over cream cheese layer. Refrigerate for 15-20 minutes or until set. Top with remaining whipped topping and pecans. Refrigerate for 1-2 hours. **Yield:** 16-20 servings.

Cream Cake Dessert

Peggy Stott, Burlington, Iowa

Folks really go for this light cake with fluffy cream filling. My son first tried this treat while in high school and asked me to get the recipe. I've used it countless times since for all sorts of occasions. It's easy to transport to a potluck because the cream is on the inside.

- 1 package (18-1/4 ounces) yellow cake mix
- 1 package (3.4 ounces) instant vanilla pudding mix
- 1/2 cup shortening
- 1 cup water
- 4 eggs

FILLING:
- 5 tablespoons all-purpose flour
- 1 cup milk
- 1/2 cup butter *or* margarine, softened
- 1/2 cup shortening
- 1 cup sugar
- 1 teaspoon vanilla extract
- 1/2 teaspoon salt

Fresh raspberries, optional

In a mixing bowl, beat cake mix, pudding mix and shortening on low speed until crumbly. Add the water and eggs; beat on medium for 2 minutes. Pour into a greased and floured 13-in. x 9-in. x 2-in. baking pan. Bake at 350° for 30-35 minutes or until a toothpick inserted near the center comes out clean. Cool for 10 minutes; invert onto a wire rack to cool completely.

Meanwhile, in a saucepan, combine flour and milk until smooth. Bring to a boil; cook and stir for 2 minutes or until thickened. Cool completely. In a mixing bowl, cream the butter, shortening, sugar, vanilla and salt; beat in milk mixture until sugar is dissolved, about 5 minutes. Split cake into two horizontal layers. Spread filling over the bottom layer; replace top layer. Cut into serving-size pieces. Garnish with raspberries if desired. **Yield:** 16-20 servings.

Summer Berry Pie

Judi Messina, Coeur d'Alene, Idaho

Mom puts luscious fresh blueberries, strawberries and raspberries to great use in this cool, refreshing pie. A super dessert on a hot day, it provides a nice light ending to a hearty meal.

- 1-1/2 cups sugar
- 6 tablespoons cornstarch
- 3 cups cold water
- 1 package (6 ounces) raspberry *or* strawberry gelatin
- 2 cups fresh blueberries
- 2 cups sliced fresh strawberries
- 2 cups fresh raspberries
- 2 graham cracker crusts (9 inches)
- 4 cups whipped topping

Fresh mint and additional sliced strawberries

In a saucepan, combine sugar, cornstarch and water until smooth. Bring to a boil; cook and stir for 2 minutes or until thickened. Remove from the heat. Stir in gelatin until dissolved. Refrigerate for 15-20 minutes or until mixture begins to thicken. Stir in the berries. Pour into crusts and chill until set. Garnish with whipped topping, mint and strawberries. **Yield:** 2 pies (6-8 servings each).

Chocolate Chip Cookie Dough Cheesecake

(Pictured below)

Julie Craig, Jackson, Wisconsin

I created this recipe to combine two of my all-time favorites—cheesecake for the grown-up in me and chocolate chip cookie dough for the little girl in me. Sour cream offsets the sweetness and adds a nice tang. Everyone who tries this scrumptious treat loves it.

- 1-3/4 cups crushed chocolate chip cookies *or* chocolate wafer crumbs
- 1/4 cup sugar
- 1/3 cup butter *or* margarine, melted

FILLING:
- 3 packages (8 ounces *each*) cream cheese, softened
- 1 cup sugar
- 3 eggs
- 1 cup (8 ounces) sour cream
- 1/2 teaspoon vanilla extract

COOKIE DOUGH:
- 1/4 cup butter *or* margarine, softened
- 1/4 cup sugar
- 1/4 cup packed brown sugar
- 1 tablespoon water
- 1 teaspoon vanilla extract
- 1/2 cup all-purpose flour
- 1-1/2 cups miniature semisweet chocolate chips, *divided*

In a small bowl, combine cookie crumbs and sugar; stir in butter. Press onto the bottom and 1 in. up the sides of a greased 9-in. springform pan; set aside.

In a mixing bowl, beat cream cheese and sugar until smooth. Add eggs; beat on low just until combined. Add sour cream and vanilla; beat just until blended. Pour over crust; set aside.

In another mixing bowl, cream butter and sugars on medium speed for 3 minutes. Add water and vanilla. Gradually add flour. Stir in 1 cup chocolate chips. Drop

dough by teaspoonfuls over filling, gently pushing dough below surface (dough should be completely covered by filling). Bake at 350° for 45-55 minutes or until center is almost set. Cool on a wire rack for 10 minutes. Carefully run a knife around edge of pan to loosen; cool 1 hour longer. Refrigerate overnight; remove sides of pan. Sprinkle with remaining chips. **Yield:** 12-14 servings.

Chocolate Orange Cookies

(Pictured above)

Ruth Rumple, Rockford, Ohio

My three sisters like the combination of chocolate and orange as much as I do, so we all really savor these beautiful cookies. The candied orange peel on top is a special twist.

- 1 cup butter *or* margarine, softened
- 3/4 cup sugar, *divided*
- 1 egg
- 1 teaspoon vanilla extract
- 2-1/2 cups all-purpose flour
- 1/2 teaspoon salt
- 1/4 cup finely grated orange peel
- 1 cup (6 ounces) semisweet chocolate chips, melted

In a mixing bowl, cream butter and 1/2 cup sugar. Add egg and vanilla. Gradually add flour and salt; mix well. Cover and chill for 15 minutes. Roll dough on a floured surface to 1/4-in. thickness. Cut with a 2-in. cookie cutter or shape into 2-in. x 1-in. rectangles. Place 2 in. apart on ungreased baking sheets. Combine orange peel and remaining sugar; spread over cookies. Bake at 350° for 14-16 minutes or until the edges just begin to brown. Remove to wire racks to cool completely. Decorate cookies with melted chocolate. **Yield:** about 3 dozen.

Frosted Banana Bars

(Pictured below)

Debbie Knight, Marion, Iowa

I make these moist bars whenever I have ripe bananas on hand, then store them in the freezer to share later at a potluck. With creamy frosting and big banana flavor, this treat is a real crowd-pleaser.

  1/2 cup butter *or* margarine, softened
1-1/2 cups sugar
  2 eggs
  1 cup (8 ounces) sour cream
  1 teaspoon vanilla extract
  2 cups all-purpose flour
  1 teaspoon baking soda
  1/4 teaspoon salt
  2 medium ripe bananas, mashed (about 1 cup)
FROSTING:
  1 package (8 ounces) cream cheese, softened
  1/2 cup butter *or* margarine, softened
  2 teaspoons vanilla extract
3-3/4 to 4 cups confectioners' sugar

In a mixing bowl, cream butter and sugar. Add eggs, sour cream and vanilla. Combine flour, baking soda and salt; gradually add to creamed mixture. Stir in bananas. Spread into a greased 15-in. x 10-in. x 1-in. baking pan. Bake at 350° for 20-25 minutes or until a toothpick inserted near center comes out clean. Cool.

For frosting, in a mixing bowl, beat cream cheese, butter and vanilla. Gradually beat in enough confectioners' sugar to achieve desired consistency. Frost bars. Store in the refrigerator. **Yield:** 3-4 dozen.

Chocolate Cherry Torte

(Pictured above)

Sue Gronholz, Columbus, Wisconsin

Mom has made this sweet treat for years. Since she knows how much my sister and I like it, she's still happy to serve this torte when we're home for a meal. The chocolate-covered graham cracker crust and fluffy filling are extra-special.

  56 chocolate-covered graham cracker cookies,
    crushed (about 1 pound)
  1 cup butter *or* margarine, melted
  2 envelopes whipped topping mix
  1 cup cold milk
  1 teaspoon vanilla extract
  1 package (8 ounces) cream cheese, softened
  2 cans (21 ounces *each*) cherry pie filling

Set aside 1/4 cup crushed cookies for topping. Combine the remaining cookies with butter; spread into a 13-in. x 9-in. x 2-in. dish. Set aside. In a mixing bowl, combine whipped topping mixes, milk and vanilla; beat on low speed until blended. Beat on high for 4 minutes or until thickened and stiff peaks form. Add cream cheese; beat until smooth. Spread over crust; top with pie filling. Sprinkle with reserved cookies. Refrigerate for 12-24 hours before serving. **Yield:** 12-16 servings.

Super Brownies

Bernice Muilenburg, Molalla, Oregon

Even though he's not a chocolate fan, my husband loves these brownies. I fix them often for my family, company and potlucks.

  1/2 cup butter *or* margarine
1-1/2 cups sugar
4-2/3 cups (28 ounces) semisweet chocolate chips,
    divided
  3 tablespoons hot water

4 eggs
5 teaspoons vanilla extract
1-1/2 cups all-purpose flour
1/2 teaspoon baking soda
1/2 teaspoon salt
2 cups coarsely chopped macadamia nuts *or* pecans, *divided*

In a saucepan over medium heat, melt butter and sugar. Remove from the heat; stir in 2 cups chocolate chips until melted. Pour into a mixing bowl; beat in water. Add eggs, one at a time, beating well after each addition. Add vanilla. Combine flour, baking soda and salt; beat into the chocolate mixture until smooth. Stir in 2 cups of chocolate chips and 1 cup of nuts.

Pour into a greased 13-in. x 9-in. x 2-in. baking pan. Sprinkle with remaining chips and nuts. Bake at 325° for 55 minutes or until the center is set (do not overbake). **Yield:** about 3-1/2 dozen.

Potluck Apple Pie

Alma Lynne Gravel, Trappe, Pennsylvania

In charge of dessert for a fund-raising dinner at our church, I experimented and came up with this scrumptious pie made in a jelly roll pan. It fed a group and got rave reviews. With flavorful apples and maple syrup, it gives a true taste of the Northeast.

2-1/4 cups all-purpose flour, *divided*
1/4 cup water
Pinch salt
1 cup shortening
FILLING:
1/2 cup maple syrup, *divided*
3 pounds tart apples (8 to 9 medium), peeled and thinly sliced
1-1/4 cups sugar
1/4 cup lemon juice
2 teaspoons ground cinnamon
1 teaspoon vanilla extract
TOPPING:
1 cup all-purpose flour
1/2 cup packed brown sugar
1/2 cup cold butter *or* margarine
1 cup chopped pecans

In a small bowl, combine 1/4 cup flour and water until smooth; set aside. In a large bowl, combine salt and remaining flour; cut in shortening until mixture resembles coarse crumbs. Add reserved flour mixture; knead gently until dough forms a ball. Press dough onto the bottom and up the sides of an ungreased 15-in. x 10-in. x 1-in. baking pan. Spread 1/4 cup syrup over crust.

Arrange apples over syrup. Combine sugar, lemon juice, cinnamon, vanilla and remaining syrup; drizzle over apples. For topping, combine flour and sugar in a bowl; cut in butter until the mixture resembles coarse crumbs. Stir in pecans. Sprinkle over filling. Bake at 350° for 1 hour or until apples are tender. **Yield:** 18-24 servings.

Editor's Note: Pastry can be easily pressed into the pan by placing a large sheet of plastic wrap on top of the dough.

English Toffee Bars

(Pictured below)

Dianne Brooks, Augusta, Kansas

My mother and I get together every year around Christmastime to make this delicious chocolate-coated toffee, using a recipe she got years ago in a cooking class. Our families and friends wait with mouths watering for their packages.

1 tablespoon plus 1-3/4 cups butter (no substitutes), softened, *divided*
2 cups sugar
1 tablespoon light corn syrup
1 cup chopped pecans
1/4 teaspoon salt
1 pound milk chocolate candy coating

Butter a 15-in. x 10-in. x 1-in. baking pan with 1 tablespoon butter; set aside. In a heavy 3-qt. saucepan, melt the remaining butter. Add sugar and corn syrup; cook and stir over medium heat until a candy thermometer reads 295° (soft-crack stage). Remove from the heat; stir in pecans and salt. Quickly pour into prepared pan. Let stand for 5 minutes.

Using a sharp knife, score into squares; cut along scored lines. Let stand at room temperature until cool. Separate into squares, using a sharp knife if necessary. In a microwave or heavy saucepan, melt milk chocolate candy coating, stirring often. Dip squares, one at a time, in coating. Place on waxed paper until set. **Yield:** 2-1/4 pounds.

Editor's Note: We recommend you test your candy thermometer before each use by bringing water to a boil; the thermometer should read 212°. Adjust your recipe temperature up or down based on your test.

Nutty Chocolate Marshmallow Puffs

Pat Ball, Abilene, Texas

We like to do things big here in Texas, so don't expect a dainty, little barely-a-bite truffle from this surprising candy recipe. Family and friends are delighted to discover a big fluffy marshmallow inside the chocolate and nut coating.

    2 cups milk chocolate chips
    1 can (14 ounces) sweetened condensed milk
    1 jar (7 ounces) marshmallow creme
    40 large marshmallows
    4 cups coarsely chopped pecans (about 1
      pound)

In a microwave or heavy saucepan, heat chocolate chips, milk and marshmallow creme just until melted; stir until smooth (mixture will be thick). With tongs, immediately dip marshmallows, one at a time, in chocolate mixture. Shake off excess chocolate; quickly roll in pecans. Place on waxed paper-lined baking sheets. (Reheat chocolate mixture if necessary for easier coating.) Refrigerate until firm. Store in the refrigerator in an airtight container. **Yield:** 40 candies.

Peanut Butter Chocolate Cake

(Pictured above)

Dorcas Yoder, Weyers Cave, Virginia

In our chocolate-loving house, slices of this cake disappears very quickly! Peanut butter is the perfect complement to the chocolate.

    2 cups all-purpose flour
    2 cups sugar
    2/3 cup baking cocoa
    2 teaspoons baking soda
    1 teaspoon baking powder
    1/2 teaspoon salt
    2 eggs
    1 cup milk
    2/3 cup vegetable oil
    1 teaspoon vanilla extract
    1 cup brewed coffee, room temperature
PEANUT BUTTER FROSTING:
    1 package (3 ounces) cream cheese, softened
    1/4 cup creamy peanut butter
    2 cups confectioners' sugar
    2 tablespoons milk
    1/2 teaspoon vanilla extract
Miniature semisweet chocolate chips, optional

In a mixing bowl, combine the flour, sugar, baking cocoa, baking soda, baking powder and salt. Add eggs, milk, oil and vanilla; beat for 2 minutes. Stir in coffee (batter will be thin). Pour into a greased 13-in. x 9-in. x 2-in. baking pan. Bake at 350° for 35-40 minutes or until a toothpick inserted near the center comes out clean. Cool completely on a wire rack.

For frosting, beat the cream cheese and peanut butter in a mixing bowl until smooth. Beat in sugar, milk and vanilla. Spread over cake. Sprinkle with chocolate chips if desired. Store in the refrigerator. **Yield:** 12-16 servings.

Chocolate Pecan Caramels

June Humphrey, Strongsville, Ohio

I haven't missed a year making this candy for the holidays since a friend gave me the recipe in 1964! It is made like a pan of upside-down bars and tastes like my favorite caramel pecan candies. I make enough to give away as gifts and keep enough for myself, too.

    1 tablespoon plus 1 cup butter (no substitutes),
      softened, *divided*
1-1/2 cups coarsely chopped pecans, toasted
    1 cup (6 ounces) semisweet chocolate chips
    2 cups packed brown sugar
    1 cup light corn syrup
    1/4 cup water
    1 can (14 ounces) sweetened condensed milk
    2 teaspoons vanilla extract

Line a 13-in. x 9-in. x 2-in. baking pan with foil; butter the foil with 1 tablespoon butter. Sprinkle with pecans and chocolate chips; set aside.

In a heavy saucepan over medium heat, melt remaining butter. Add brown sugar, corn syrup and water. Cook and stir until mixture comes to a boil. Stir in milk. Cook, stirring constantly, until a candy thermometer reads 248° (firm-ball stage). Remove from heat and stir in vanilla.

Pour into prepared pan (do not scrape saucepan). Cool completely before cutting. **Yield:** about 2-1/2 pounds (about 6-3/4 dozen).

Editor's Note: We recommend that you test your candy thermometer before each use by bringing water to a boil; the thermometer should read 212°. Adjust your recipe temperature up or down based on your test.

Rhubarb Elderberry Crisp

(Pictured above)

Carolyn Scouten, Wyalusing, Pennsylvania

Rhubarb and elderberries are quite abundant around these parts, so I combined the two in this wonderful crisp. It's been well received by our friends, who always ask for the recipe.

    1 cup all-purpose flour
  3/4 cup quick-cooking oats
1-1/2 cups sugar, *divided*
    1 teaspoon ground cinnamon
  1/2 cup cold butter *or* margarine
    3 cups diced rhubarb
    2 cups elderberries *or* blackberries
    2 tablespoons cornstarch
    1 cup water
    1 teaspoon vanilla extract

In a bowl, combine the flour, oats, 1/2 cup sugar and cinnamon; cut in butter until mixture resembles coarse crumbs. Set aside half for topping. Press remaining crumb mixture into an ungreased 11-in. x 7-in. x 2-in. baking dish. Top with rhubarb and berries.
In a small saucepan, combine cornstarch and remaining sugar. Gradually stir in water; bring to a boil. Reduce heat; cook and stir for 1-2 minutes or until thickened. Remove from the heat; stir in vanilla. Pour over the fruit. Sprinkle with the reserved crumb mixture. Bake at 350° for 50-55 minutes or until golden brown. Serve warm or cold. **Yield:** 10 servings.

Take the Cake

TO KEEP a cake from sliding on its plate during transit, drizzle a bit of frosting in a circle on the plate where the cake will rest. The frosting will hold the cake in place, and your dessert will arrive in perfect shape.

Sunflower Potluck Cake

(Pictured below)

Lola Wiemer, Clarklake, Michigan

I wish I knew who to thank for the idea for my cake. I first saw it on the dessert table at a picnic. Later, for something different, I did my own variation. As a minister's wife for over 60 years, I have tried many new dishes!

  3/4 cup butter *or* margarine, softened
1-2/3 cups sugar
    3 eggs
    1 teaspoon vanilla extract
    2 cups all-purpose flour
  2/3 cup baking cocoa
1-1/4 teaspoons baking soda
    1 teaspoon salt
  1/4 teaspoon baking powder
1-1/3 cups water
    1 cup prepared chocolate frosting, *divided*
    1 cup (6 ounces) semisweet chocolate chips
   22 cream-filled sponge cakes
    1 teaspoon milk
    2 craft decorating bees, optional

In a mixing bowl, cream butter and sugar. Add eggs, one at a time, beating well after each addition. Add vanilla. Combine dry ingredients; add to the creamed mixture alternately with water. Pour into two greased and floured 9-in. round cake pans. Bake at 350° for 25-30 minutes or until a toothpick inserted near the center comes out clean. Cool in pans for 10 minutes; remove to wire racks and cool completely. Freeze one layer for future use.
Set aside 1 tablespoon frosting. Frost top and sides of remaining cake. Place cake in the center of a large round tray (about 18 in.). Arrange chocolate chips on top of cake. Place sponge cakes around cake. Mix reserved frosting with milk; drizzle over sponge cakes. Decorate with bees if desired. **Yield:** 22 servings.

Butterscotch Pecan Slices

(Pictured above)

Esther Thys, Belle Plaine, Iowa

I love the rich, buttery flavor these crisp cookies get from pecans and brown sugar. Once the dough is in the refrigerator, I can have freshly baked cookies in just minutes. For a gathering or when company drops in, I'm prepared with a tasty treat.

    6 tablespoons butter *or* margarine, softened
  2/3 cup packed brown sugar
    1 egg
  1/2 teaspoon vanilla extract
1-1/4 cups all-purpose flour
  1/2 teaspoon baking powder
  1/4 teaspoon salt
  3/4 cup finely chopped pecans, *divided*

In a mixing bowl, cream the butter and brown sugar. Beat in egg and vanilla. Combine flour, baking powder and salt; gradually add to the creamed mixture. Stir in 1/2 cup pecans. Shape into two 7-in. rolls; wrap each in plastic wrap. Refrigerate for 2 hours or until firm. Unwrap and cut into 1/4-in. slices. Place 2 in. apart on ungreased baking sheets. Sprinkle with remaining nuts; press gently. Bake at 350° for 10-12 minutes or until edges begin to brown. **Yield:** 4 dozen.

Buttermilk Banana Cake

Arlene Grenz, Linton, North Dakota

When I was a girl, this was my family's favorite Sunday cake. Since I'm "nuts" about nuts, I added the pecans. It became our youngsters' favorite as well.

  3/4 cup butter *or* margarine, softened
    1 cup sugar
  1/2 cup packed brown sugar

    2 eggs
    1 cup mashed ripe banana
    1 teaspoon vanilla extract
    2 cups cake flour
    1 teaspoon baking powder
    1 teaspoon baking soda
  1/2 teaspoon salt
  1/2 cup buttermilk
FILLING/FROSTING:
  1/2 cup half-and-half cream
  1/2 cup sugar
    2 tablespoons butter *or* margarine
    2 tablespoons all-purpose flour
  1/4 teaspoon salt
    1 teaspoon vanilla extract
  1/2 cup chopped pecans
    2 cups whipping cream
  1/4 cup confectioners' sugar

In a mixing bowl, cream butter and sugars until fluffy. Add eggs; beat for 2 minutes. Add banana and vanilla; beat for 2 minutes. Combine the flour, baking powder, baking soda and salt; add to creamed mixture alternately with buttermilk. Pour into two greased and floured 9-in. round cake pans. Bake at 375° for 25-30 minutes or until a toothpick inserted near the center comes out clean. Cool in pans 10 minutes; remove to wire racks and cool completely.

For filling, combine half-and-half, sugar, butter, flour and salt in a saucepan. Bring to a boil; cook and stir for 2 minutes. Remove from the heat; stir in vanilla and pecans. Cool. Spread between cake layers. For frosting, beat whipping cream until soft peaks form. Gradually beat in the confectioners' sugar; beat until stiff peaks form. Spread over top and sides of cake. Store in the refrigerator. **Yield:** 12-16 servings.

Cranberry Date Bars

Mrs. Richard Grams, La Crosse, Wisconsin

I enjoy making this when the cranberry season arrives. It's very easy to put together, which is perfect for busy moms like me.

    1 package (12 ounces) fresh *or* frozen
      cranberries
    1 package (8 ounces) chopped dates
    1 teaspoon vanilla extract
    2 cups all-purpose flour
    2 cups quick-cooking oats
1-1/2 cups packed brown sugar
  1/2 teaspoon baking soda
  1/4 teaspoon salt
    1 cup butter *or* margarine, melted
ORANGE GLAZE:
    2 cups confectioners' sugar
    2 to 3 tablespoons orange juice
  1/2 teaspoon vanilla extract

In a saucepan, combine cranberries and dates. Cover and cook over low heat for 15 minutes or until berries pop, stirring often. Remove from the heat and stir in vanilla; set aside. In a bowl, combine flour, oats, sugar, baking soda and salt. Stir in butter until crumbly. Press half into an ungreased 13-in. x 9-in. x 2-in. baking pan.

Bake at 350° for 8 minutes. Spoon cranberry mixture over the crust; spread gently. Sprinkle with remaining crumb mixture; pat down gently. Bake at 350° for 20-25 minutes or until golden brown. Cool. Combine glaze ingredients; drizzle over bars. **Yield:** 4 dozen.

Almond Plum Kuchen

(Pictured below)

Norma Enders, Edmonton, Alberta

You'll find this dessert both easy and very tasty. Everyone who tries it comments on how the orange and plum flavors go together so well and complement each other. We like it best when it is served warm with ice cream on top.

1-1/2 cups all-purpose flour
3/4 cup packed brown sugar
1/2 cup ground almonds
1 tablespoon grated orange peel
3/4 cup cold butter *or* margarine
FILLING:
3 eggs
3/4 cup sugar
1/2 cup all-purpose flour
1/2 cup ground almonds
1 tablespoon grated orange peel
1/2 teaspoon baking powder
7 to 8 cups quartered fresh plums
TOPPING:
1/4 cup sugar
1/4 cup all-purpose flour
1/4 cup butter *or* margarine, softened
1/2 cup sliced almonds

In a bowl, combine the first four ingredients; cut in butter until the mixture resembles coarse crumbs. Press into a greased 13-in. x 9-in. x 2-in. baking dish. Bake at 375° for 15 minutes. Meanwhile, in a mixing bowl, beat eggs and sugar until thick and lemon-colored, about 5 minutes. Stir in flour, almonds, orange peel and baking powder. Arrange plums over crust; pour egg mixture over plums. Combine the first three topping ingredients; sprinkle over filling. Top with almonds. Bake for 40-45 minutes or until golden brown. **Yield:** 12 servings.

Devil's Food Sheet Cake

(Pictured above)

James Crabb, Greeley, Colorado

I like this cake because it's so moist and rich. It's great for large gatherings because it's so easy to make.

1-1/2 cups water
2 cups sugar
3/4 cup butter *or* margarine
2 eggs, lightly beaten
1 teaspoon vanilla extract
2 cups all-purpose flour
1/2 cup baking cocoa
2 teaspoons baking soda
1/2 teaspoon salt
FROSTING:
1/4 cup butter *or* margarine, softened
2 cups confectioners' sugar
2 tablespoons baking cocoa
1/2 teaspoon vanilla extract
2 to 3 tablespoons milk

In a large saucepan, bring water to a boil. Remove from the heat. Stir in sugar and butter until butter is melted. Add eggs and vanilla; mix well. Combine flour, cocoa, baking soda and salt; add to butter mixture and mix thoroughly. Pour into a greased and floured 15-in. x 10-in. x 1-in. baking pan. Bake at 350° for 30-35 minutes or until a toothpick inserted near the center comes out clean. Cool completely on a wire rack.

For frosting, beat butter, confectioners' sugar, cocoa, vanilla and enough milk to reach a spreading consistency. Frost cake. **Yield:** 16-20 servings.

tioners' sugar until smooth. Add whipped topping; mix well. Spread over crust. Arrange fruit on top. Combine glaze ingredients in a saucepan; bring to a boil, stirring constantly. Boil for 2 minutes or until thickened. Cool to room temperature, about 30 minutes. Brush over fruit. Store in the refrigerator. **Yield:** 12-16 servings.

Summer Dessert Pizza

(Pictured above)

Ida Ruth Wenger, Harrisonburg, Virginia

My family enjoys this dessert anytime of the year, but it's especially refreshing during the hot months. You can use whatever fruits are in season.

    1/4 cup butter *or* margarine, softened
    1/2 cup sugar
      1 egg
    1/4 teaspoon vanilla extract
    1/4 teaspoon lemon extract
  1-1/4 cups all-purpose flour
    1/4 teaspoon baking powder
    1/4 teaspoon baking soda
    1/4 teaspoon salt
      4 ounces cream cheese, softened
    1/4 cup confectioners' sugar
      1 cup whipped topping
      1 firm banana, sliced
      1 cup sliced fresh strawberries
      1 can (8 ounces) mandarin oranges, drained
      2 kiwifruit, peeled and thinly sliced
    1/3 cup fresh blueberries
GLAZE:
    1/4 cup sugar
    1/4 cup orange juice
    1/4 cup water
      2 teaspoons cornstarch

In a mixing bowl, cream butter and sugar; beat in egg and extracts. Combine flour, baking powder, baking soda and salt; add to creamed mixture. Beat well. Cover and chill for 30 minutes. Press dough into a greased 12-in. or 14-in. pizza pan. Bake at 350° for 12-14 minutes or until light golden brown. Cool completely.

In a mixing bowl, beat cream cheese and confec-

Pumpkin Pound Cake

Virginia Loew, Leesburg, Florida

This cake is perfect for fall. As it bakes, the aroma fills the house with a spicy scent.

  2-1/2 cups sugar
      1 cup vegetable oil
      3 eggs
      3 cups all-purpose flour
      2 teaspoons baking soda
      1 teaspoon ground cinnamon
      1 teaspoon ground nutmeg
    1/2 teaspoon salt
    1/4 teaspoon ground cloves
      1 can (15 ounces) solid-pack pumpkin
Confectioners' sugar

In a mixing bowl, blend sugar and oil. Add eggs, one at a time, beating well after each addition. Combine flour, baking soda, cinnamon, nutmeg, salt and cloves; add to egg mixture alternately with pumpkin. Transfer to a greased 12-cup fluted tube pan. Bake at 350° for 60-65 minutes or until a toothpick inserted near the center comes out clean. Cool for 10 minutes before inverting onto a wire rack. Remove pan and cool completely. Dust with confectioners' sugar. **Yield:** 12-16 servings.

Zucchini Chip Cupcakes

Debra Forshee, Stockton, Kansas

My three girls love these moist, nut-topped cupcakes even without frosting. They're a great way to use up zucchini, and they freeze well for a quick snack.

    1/2 cup butter *or* margarine, softened
    1/2 cup vegetable oil
  1-3/4 cups sugar
      2 eggs
    1/2 cup milk
      1 teaspoon vanilla extract
  2-1/2 cups all-purpose flour
    1/4 cup baking cocoa
      1 teaspoon baking soda
    1/2 teaspoon salt
    1/2 teaspoon ground cinnamon
      2 cups shredded zucchini
    1/4 cup miniature semisweet chocolate chips
    1/4 cup chopped pecans

In a mixing bowl, cream butter, oil and sugar. Add eggs, milk and vanilla; mix well. Combine flour, cocoa, baking soda, salt and cinnamon; add to the creamed mixture. Fold in zucchini and chocolate chips. Fill greased or paper-lined muffin cups two-thirds full. Top with pecans. Bake at 375° for 20-25 minutes or until top springs back when lightly touched. **Yield:** about 2 dozen.

Marbled Chocolate Cheesecake Bars

(Pictured below)

Elaine Hanson, Waite Park, Minnesota

I learned to bake and cook from my mother. I grew up in a family of 12 and we all had chores to do—mine was to help prepare the meals. The more I cooked, the more I enjoyed it. Now it's my favorite hobby.

   3/4 cup water
   1/2 cup butter (no substitutes)
1-1/2 squares (1-1/2 ounces) unsweetened chocolate
   2 cups all-purpose flour
1-1/2 cups packed brown sugar
   1 teaspoon baking soda
   1/2 teaspoon salt
   2 eggs
   1/2 cup sour cream
CREAM CHEESE MIXTURE:
   1 package (8 ounces) cream cheese, softened
   1/3 cup sugar
   1 egg, beaten
   1 tablespoon vanilla extract
   1 cup (6 ounces) semisweet chocolate chips

In a small saucepan, combine water, butter and chocolate; cook and stir over low heat until smooth. Cool. In a mixing bowl, combine flour, brown sugar, baking soda and salt. Add eggs and sour cream; beat on low just until combined. Stir in chocolate mixture until smooth.

In another bowl, beat cream cheese, sugar, egg and vanilla; set aside. Spread chocolate batter into a greased 15-in. x 10-in. x 1-in. baking pan. Drop cream cheese mixture by tablespoonfuls over batter; cut through the batter with a knife to swirl. Sprinkle with

chocolate chips. Bake at 375° for 20-25 minutes or until a toothpick inserted near the center comes out clean. Cool on a wire rack. **Yield:** about 6 dozen.

Fresh Fruit Cobbler

(Pictured above)

Paula Chick, Lewiston, Maine

I received this recipe years ago. It's a family favorite, especially when Maine blueberries are in season. What a treat to eat on a hot summer day!

   5 to 6 cups chopped fresh fruit (apples, rhubarb, blueberries *or* peaches)*
   2 cups all-purpose flour
   1/2 cup sugar
   4 teaspoons baking powder
   1 teaspoon salt
   1/2 cup butter *or* margarine
   1 cup milk
TOPPING:
   2/3 cup sugar
   1/4 cup cornstarch
1-1/2 cups boiling water

Arrange fruit evenly in the bottom of a 13-in. x 9-in. x 2-in. greased baking pan. In a bowl, combine flour, sugar, baking powder and salt; cut in butter until crumbly. Stir in milk. Spoon over fruit. Combine sugar and cornstarch; sprinkle over batter. Pour water over all. Bake at 350° for 40-45 minutes or until fruit is tender. **Yield:** 12-16 servings.

  *Editor's Note: If desired, a combination of apples and rhubarb or blueberries and peaches can be used.

Cheesecake Squares

(Pictured above)

Shirley Forest, Eau Claire, Wisconsin

I lived on a dairy farm when I was young and my mom always had a lot of sour cream to use. She never wasted any, and this cheesecake was one of my family's favorites. It's great topped with blackberry sauce.

      2 packages (8 ounces *each*) cream cheese,
        softened
      1 cup ricotta cheese
  1-1/2 cups sugar
      4 eggs
    1/4 cup butter *or* margarine, melted and cooled
      3 tablespoons cornstarch
      3 tablespoons all-purpose flour
      1 tablespoon vanilla extract
      2 cups (16 ounces) sour cream
Seasonal fresh fruit, optional

In a mixing bowl, beat cream cheese, ricotta and sugar until smooth. Add the eggs, one at a time, mixing well after each addition. Add butter, cornstarch, flour and vanilla; beat until smooth. Fold in sour cream. Pour into a greased 13-in. x 9-in. x 2-in. baking pan. Bake, uncovered, at 325° for 1 hour. Do not open oven door. Turn oven off. Let cheesecake stand in closed oven for 2 hours. Cool completely on a wire rack. Chill several hours or overnight. Top each square with fruit if desired. **Yield:** 20 servings.

Zucchini Dessert Squares

Nancy Morelli, Livonia, Michigan

We planted one too many zucchini plants a few summers ago and harvested a lot of zucchinis that year. I was looking for ways to use them...this delicious dessert is the result.

      4 cups all-purpose flour
      2 cups sugar
    1/2 teaspoon ground cinnamon
    1/2 teaspoon salt
  1-1/2 cups cold butter *or* margarine
FILLING:
      8 to 10 cups cubed seeded peeled zucchini
        (4 to 5 pounds)
    2/3 cup lemon juice
      1 cup sugar
      1 teaspoon ground cinnamon
    1/2 teaspoon ground nutmeg

In a bowl, combine flour, sugar, cinnamon and salt. Cut in butter until crumbly; reserve 3 cups. Pat remaining crumb mixture into the bottom of a greased 13-in. x 9-in. x 2-in. baking pan. Bake at 375° for 12 minutes.

Meanwhile, for filling, place zucchini and lemon juice in a saucepan; bring to a boil. Reduce heat; cover and cook for 6-8 minutes or until zucchini is crisp-tender. Stir in sugar, cinnamon and nutmeg; cover. Simmer for 5 minutes (mixture will be thin). Spoon over crust; sprinkle with reserved crumb mixture. Bake at 375° for 40-45 minutes or until golden. **Yield:** 16-20 servings.

Raspberry Marshmallow Delight

(Pictured below)

Gloria Iden, Kimmell, Indiana

This is one of our family's favorite desserts. It has a tangy, unique flavor. After a hard day of working on the

farm, this fruity treat is most welcome. It's a good addition to a potluck table.

 1-1/4 cups graham cracker crumbs
  1/4 cup butter *or* margarine, melted
   50 large marshmallows
    1 cup milk
    1 carton (8 ounces) frozen whipped topping,
      thawed
    2 packages (10 ounces *each*) frozen raspberries
      in syrup, thawed
 1-1/4 cups water, *divided*
  1/2 cup sugar
    2 teaspoons lemon juice
    6 tablespoons cornstarch
Whipped cream and fresh raspberries, optional

Combine crumbs and butter; press into the bottom of a greased 13-in. x 9-in. 2-in. baking pan. Bake at 350° for 10 minutes. Cool. In a large saucepan over medium heat, stir marshmallows and milk until the marshmallows are melted. Cool to room temperature. Fold in whipped topping; spread over crust.

In a saucepan, bring raspberries, 1 cup water, sugar and lemon juice to a boil. Combine cornstarch and remaining water; stir into raspberry mixture. Boil for 2 minutes, stirring constantly. Cool to room temperature. Spread over marshmallow layer. Chill until firm, about 4 hours. Garnish with whipped cream and raspberries if desired. **Yield:** 12-16 servings.

Triple-Fudge Brownies

Denise Nebel, Wayland, Iowa

When you're in a hurry to make dessert, here's a "mix of mixes" that's so convenient and quick. The result is a big pan of very rich, fudgy brownies. Friends who ask me for the recipe are amazed that it's so easy.

    1 package (3.9 ounces) instant chocolate
      pudding mix
    1 package (18-1/4 ounces) chocolate cake mix
    2 cups (12 ounces) semisweet chocolate chips
Confectioners' sugar
Vanilla ice cream, optional

Prepare pudding according to package directions. Whisk in cake mix. Stir in chocolate chips. Pour into a greased 15-in. x 10-in. x 1-in. baking pan. Bake at 350° for 30-35 minutes or until the top springs back when lightly touched. Dust with confectioners' sugar. Serve with ice cream if desired. **Yield:** 4 dozen.

Fast Frosting

AFTER removing a pan of brownies from the oven, sprinkle with chocolate chips. Let stand until the chocolate melts. Spread with a rubber spatula.

Strawberry Banana Trifle

(Pictured above)

Kim Waterhouse, Randolph, Maine

No matter where I take this impressive-looking dessert, the bowl gets emptied in minutes. It's fun to make because everyone always "oohs" and "ahhs" over how pretty it is.

    1 cup sugar
  1/4 cup cornstarch
    3 tablespoons strawberry gelatin powder
    1 cup cold water
    1 pint fresh strawberries, sliced
 1-3/4 cups cold milk
    1 package (3.4 ounces) instant vanilla pudding
      mix
    3 medium firm bananas, sliced
    1 tablespoon lemon juice
    6 cups cubed angel food cake
    2 cups whipping cream, whipped
Additional strawberries *or* banana slices, optional

In a saucepan, combine the sugar, cornstarch and gelatin; stir in water until smooth. Bring to a boil; cook and stir for 2 minutes or until thickened. Remove from the heat. Stir in strawberries; set aside.

In a mixing bowl, combine milk and pudding mix. Beat on low speed for 2 minutes; set aside. Toss bananas with lemon juice; drain and set aside. Place half of the cake cubes in a trifle bowl or 3-qt. serving bowl. Layer with half of the pudding, bananas, strawberry sauce and whipped cream. Repeat layers. Cover and refrigerate for at least 2 hours. Garnish with additional fruit if desired. **Yield:** 14 servings.

Feeding 50
Or More

Raspberry Truffle
Brownies (p. 103)

Chapter 8

Party Potato Salad

Dona Sundsmo, Tacoma, Washington

This potato salad has been a staple for me for years. A friend and I prepared enough to serve 200 guests at my oldest son's wedding reception.

10 pounds potatoes, peeled and cubed
3 cups mayonnaise
3 cups sweet pickle relish
2 cups chopped onion
1/2 cup prepared mustard
1 tablespoon salt
1 teaspoon pepper
15 hard-cooked eggs, chopped

Cook potatoes in boiling water until tender; drain. Combine mayonnaise, relish, onion, mustard, salt and pepper; mix well. Add eggs and warm potatoes; toss gently. Cover and refrigerate. **Yield:** 60 (1/2-cup) servings.

Sloppy Joes for 100

Linda Cailteux, Clifton, Illinois

This is a delicious, easy-to-serve main dish perfect for any large gathering where a hearty meal is in order. I use this recipe at a church dinner every year and we always sell out.

20 pounds ground beef
4 large onions, chopped
4 large green peppers, chopped
4 cups chopped celery
1 cup packed brown sugar
1 cup spicy brown mustard
4 cups ketchup
2 cans (12 ounces *each*) tomato paste
4 cans (15 ounces *each*) tomato sauce
6 to 8 cups water
1 cup vinegar
2/3 cup Worcestershire sauce
100 hamburger buns

In a large Dutch oven, cook the beef, onions, peppers and celery in batches until meat is no longer pink. Remove with a slotted spoon to a large roaster; add the next eight ingredients. Cover and simmer for 3-4 hours. Serve on buns. **Yield:** 100 servings (12 quarts).

Scalloped Carrots

Cheryl Holland, Ortonville, Michigan

This recipe is one my mom came up with. It's a real crowd-pleasing side dish with a comforting sauce and golden crumb topping.

1-1/2 cups butter *or* margarine
1-1/2 cups all-purpose flour
3 quarts milk
1/2 cup lemon juice
4 teaspoons celery salt
2 teaspoons salt

2 teaspoons pepper
6 pounds carrots, diced and cooked
2-1/2 pounds shredded cheddar cheese
6 cups crushed butter-flavored crackers

In a saucepan over medium heat, cook and stir butter and flour until smooth and bubbly, about 2 minutes. Gradually add milk and lemon juice; cook and stir until thickened. Add celery salt, salt and pepper; mix well. Remove from the heat. In four greased 2-1/2-qt. baking dishes, layer half of the carrots, sauce, cheese and crackers. Repeat layers. Bake, uncovered, at 350° for 45-50 minutes or until top is golden brown. Serve immediately. **Yield:** 50 servings.

Dipped Gingersnaps

(Pictured above)

Laura Kimball, West Jordan, Utah

I get a great deal of satisfaction making and giving time-tested treats like these soft, chewy cookies, especially at Christmas. Dipping them in white chocolate makes great gingersnaps even more special.

2 cups sugar
1-1/2 cups vegetable oil
2 eggs
1/2 cup molasses
4 cups all-purpose flour
4 teaspoons baking soda
1 tablespoon ground ginger
2 teaspoons ground cinnamon
1 teaspoon salt
Additional sugar
2 packages (10 to 12 ounces *each*) vanilla *or* white chips
1/4 cup shortening

In a mixing bowl, combine sugar and oil; mix well. Add eggs, one at a time, beating well after each addition. Stir in molasses. Combine dry ingredients; gradually add to creamed mixture and mix well. Shape into 3/4-in. balls and roll in sugar. Place 2 in. apart on ungreased baking sheets. Bake at 350° for 10-12 minutes or until cookie springs back when touched lightly. Remove to wire racks to cool.

Melt chips with shortening in a small saucepan over low heat. Dip the cookies halfway; shake off excess. Place on waxed paper-lined baking sheets to harden. **Yield:** about 14-1/2 dozen.

Beef Tips on Rice

Kathy Berndt, El Campo, Texas

Don't just rely on simple sandwiches when feeding a crowd. This is an easy, elegant main dish with tender pieces of beef.

- 20 pounds beef stew meat, cut into 1-inch cubes
- 2 tablespoons salt
- 5 teaspoons pepper
- 5 teaspoons dried thyme
- 15 cans (10-3/4 ounces *each*) condensed cream of mushroom soup, undiluted
- 4 cups water
- 4 cups chopped onion
- 2/3 cup chopped fresh parsley
- 2-1/2 teaspoons browning sauce, optional
- 6-1/2 to 7 pounds long grain rice, cooked

Combine beef, salt, pepper and thyme; mix well. Place in five greased 13-in. x 9-in. x 2-in. baking pans. Bake, uncovered, at 400° for 15 minutes; stir. Bake 15 minutes longer; drain. Combine the soup, water, onion, parsley and browning sauce if desired. Pour over beef; mix well. Cover and bake at 350° for 1-1/2 to 2 hours or until the beef is tender. Serve over rice. **Yield:** 75 servings (3/4 cup rice and 3/4 cup beef with sauce).

Family Gathering Potatoes

Sara Yoder, Mt. Hope, Ohio

This delicious Amish side dish always wins raves. Almost everyone comes back for seconds—or thirds!

- 4 cans (10-3/4 ounces *each*) condensed cream of celery soup, undiluted
- 4 cans (10-3/4 ounces *each*) condensed cream of chicken soup, undiluted
- 2 pounds process American cheese, cubed
- 4 cups (32 ounces) sour cream
- 1-1/3 cups butter *or* margarine, *divided*
- 4 teaspoons seasoned salt
- 2 teaspoons garlic powder
- 2 teaspoons pepper
- 20 pounds potatoes, peeled, cubed and cooked
- 2 cups crushed Club crackers (about 40)

In four Dutch ovens or soup kettles, combine soups, cheese, sour cream, 1 cup butter, seasoned salt, garlic powder and pepper. Cook and stir until cheese is melted and mixture is smooth. Add potatoes; mix well.

Transfer to four greased 13-in. x 9-in. x 2-in. baking

dishes (dishes will be full). Bake, uncovered, at 350° for 45-60 minutes or until bubbly. Melt remaining butter; toss with the cracker crumbs. Sprinkle over the potatoes. Bake 10-15 minutes longer or until topping is lightly browned. Let stand for 5 minutes before serving. **Yield:** 60-65 servings.

Sunflower Slaw

Betty Thompson, St. Charles, Missouri

My coleslaw combines a tangy dressing with crisp cabbage, slivered almonds, sunflower kernels and ramen noodles. It is a favorite at church suppers.

- 6 packages (3 ounces *each*) ramen noodles
- 2 packages (2-1/4 ounces *each*) slivered almonds
- 1-1/3 cups sunflower kernels
- 1/2 cup butter *or* margarine, melted
- 3-1/2 cups vegetable oil
- 2 cups vinegar
- 2 cups sugar
- 1/2 cup soy sauce
- 2 teaspoons salt
- 10 pounds cabbage, shredded

Break noodles into small pieces (save seasoning envelopes for another use). Place noodles, almonds and sunflower kernels in a 15-in. x 10-in. x 1-in. baking pan. Drizzle with butter; mix well. Bake at 350° for 8-10 minutes or until lightly browned, stirring several times; set aside. Combine oil, vinegar, sugar, soy sauce and salt; toss with cabbage. Cover and refrigerate for at least 1 hour. Stir in noodle mixture just before serving. Serve with a slotted spoon. **Yield:** 66 (3/4-cup) servings.

Stroganoff for a Crowd

Ada Lower, Minot, North Dakota

This economical, enjoyable entree is perfect when serving a crowd.

- 20 pounds ground beef
- 5 large onions, chopped
- 7 cans (26 ounces *each*) condensed cream of mushroom soup, undiluted
- 3 quarts milk
- 1/2 cup Worcestershire sauce
- 3 tablespoons garlic powder
- 2 tablespoons salt
- 1 tablespoon pepper
- 1 teaspoon paprika
- 5 pints sour cream
Hot cooked noodles

In several large stockpots, cook beef and onions until meat is no longer pink; drain. Combine soup, milk, Worcestershire sauce, garlic powder, salt, pepper and paprika; add to beef mixture. Bring to a boil; reduce heat. Just before serving, stir in sour cream; heat through but do not boil. Serve over noodles. **Yield:** 70 (1-cup) servings.

Tapioca Pudding

Bernice Hartje, Cavalier, North Dakota

The best thing about this creamy, old-fashioned pudding is that it's made the night before. That's a real plus when cooking for a crowd.

- 4 packages (3 ounces *each*) tapioca pudding mix
- 4 cups milk
- 1 carton (16 ounces) frozen whipped topping, thawed
- 2 cans (22 ounces *each*) lemon pie filling
- 1 package (10-1/2 ounces) colored *or* white miniature marshmallows
- 4 cans (17 ounces *each*) fruit cocktail, drained
- 4 cans (15 ounces *each*) mandarin oranges, drained
- 1 can (20 ounces) crushed pineapple, drained

In a large saucepan, cook pudding and milk according to package directions; cool. In a large bowl, fold whipped topping into pie filling. Add the remaining ingredients; stir gently. Fold in pudding. Refrigerate overnight. **Yield:** 70-80 servings.

Ham Salad Sandwiches

Pat Keuther, Denver, Colorado

Sweet pickles give my ham salad sandwiches a bold flavor that's irresistible. They're excellent for a ladies' luncheon.

- 4 pounds fully cooked ham *or* ring bologna, coarsely ground
- 3 cups chopped sweet pickles
- 2 cups mayonnaise *or* salad dressing
- 1 jar (2 ounces) diced pimientos, drained
- 100 slices of bread

Lettuce leaves, optional

Combine ham, pickles, mayonnaise and pimientos; mix well. Spoon 1/4 cup onto 50 slices of bread; top with lettuce if desired and remaining bread. **Yield:** 50 servings.

Stew for a Crowd

Mike Marratzo, Florence, Alabama

Need a no-fuss feast to feed a crowd? With lots of meat and vegetables, this big-batch stew is sure to satisfy the heartiest of appetites.

- 25 pounds beef stew meat
- 5 pounds onions, diced (about 16 cups)
- 2 celery stalks, cut into 1-inch pieces (about 14 cups)

About 5 quarts water
- 1/2 cup browning sauce, optional
- 1/4 cup salt
- 3 tablespoons garlic powder
- 3 tablespoons dried thyme
- 3 tablespoons seasoned salt
- 2 tablespoons pepper
- 12 bay leaves
- 15 pounds red potatoes, cut into 1-inch cubes (about 16 cups)
- 10 pounds carrots, cut into 1-inch pieces (about 24 cups)
- 10 cups frozen peas
- 10 cups frozen corn
- 4 cups all-purpose flour
- 3 to 4 cups milk

Divide the stew meat, onions and celery between several large stockpots. Add water to fill pots half full. Add browning sauce if desired and all of the seasonings. Cover and simmer for about 1-1/2 hours or until the meat is tender.

Add potatoes and carrots; simmer for 40 minutes or until vegetables are tender. Add peas and corn; simmer 1 hour longer. Combine flour and enough milk to make a smooth (not runny) paste; add to stew, stirring constantly, until thickened. Remove bay leaves before serving. **Yield:** 120 (1-cup) servings.

Vanilla Fruit Salad

Geraldine Grisdale, Mt. Pleasant, Michigan

I often serve this simple-to-make fruit salad as a side dish with a variety of main courses. But it has a nice sweet taste, which also makes it perfect for dessert. Either way, it's always well received.

- 5 cans (20 ounces *each*) pineapple chunks in juice
- 1 can (8 ounces) pineapple chunks in juice
- 4 packages (5.1 ounces *each*) instant vanilla pudding mix
- 8 cans (15 ounces *each*) mandarin oranges, drained
- 10 medium red apples, chopped

Drain pineapple, reserving juice. Add enough water to juice to make 6 cups. Place pudding in a large bowl; stir in pineapple juice until thickened, about 4-6 minutes. Fold in pineapple, oranges and apples. Pour about 8 cups each into four greased 13-in. x 9-in. x 2-in. pans. Chill until serving. **Yield:** 64 (1/2-cup) servings.

French Toast for 90

Kathleen Hall, Lakeview, Oregon

People are sometimes shocked when I say I'll bring french toast to feed a crowd. But this oven-baked version, which is prepared the night before, couldn't be easier to make and serve.

- 9 unsliced loaves (1 pound *each*) day-old French bread
- 9 dozen eggs
- 2-1/2 gallons milk
- 2 cups sugar
- 1 cup vanilla extract
- 2 tablespoons salt

GLAZE:

GLAZE:
1/4 cup semisweet chocolate chips
1 teaspoon shortening

In a heavy saucepan, melt butter and chocolate chips over low heat. Cool slightly. In a large bowl, beat eggs and brown sugar. Dissolve coffee crystals in water; add to egg mixture with melted chocolate. Mix well. Combine baking powder and flour; stir into chocolate mixture. Spread in a greased 9-in. square baking pan. Bake at 350° for 30-35 minutes or until brownies test done. Cool.

For filling, melt chocolate chips; cool. In a mixing bowl, beat cream cheese until fluffy; add confectioners' sugar and jam. Stir in melted chocolate; spread over cooled brownies. For glaze, melt chocolate chips and shortening. Drizzle over filling. Chill before cutting. Store in the refrigerator. **Yield:** about 5 dozen.

Golden Cheese Soup

Marilyn Hillam, Brigham City, Utah

This is my adaptation of a recipe served at a popular local restaurant. The large serving size comes in handy for large family gatherings and church socials.

2-1/2 cups chopped onion
1-1/4 cups butter *or* margarine
1-1/4 cups all-purpose flour
1-1/4 cups cornstarch
2-1/2 teaspoons paprika
5 teaspoons salt
2-1/2 teaspoons pepper
5 quarts chicken broth
5 quarts milk
5 cups chopped carrots, cooked
5 cups chopped celery, cooked
10 cups (2-1/2 pounds) shredded sharp cheddar cheese
2-1/2 cups chopped fresh parsley

In a large Dutch oven over medium heat, saute onion in butter until tender. Combine flour, cornstarch, paprika, salt and pepper; stir into pan until a smooth paste forms. Gradually add broth, stirring constantly. Bring to a boil; cook and stir for 2 minutes or until thickened. Gradually add milk, stirring constantly. Add carrots, celery and cheese. Cook and stir over low heat until cheese is melted and soup is heated through. Add parsley just before serving. **Yield:** 50 (1-cup) servings.

1 pound butter *or* margarine, melted
Confectioners' sugar

Slice bread into 3/4-in. pieces; arrange in 18 greased 13-in. x 9-in. x 2-in. baking dishes. Beat eggs; add milk, sugar, vanilla and salt. Mix well. Pour about 3 cups over bread in each pan. Cover and chill 8 hours or overnight. Remove from refrigerator 30 minutes before baking. Brush with butter. Bake, uncovered, at 350° for 55-65 minutes or until a knife inserted near the center comes out clean. Let stand 5 minutes. Dust with confectioners' sugar. **Yield:** 90 servings (2 slices each).

Raspberry Truffle Brownies

(Pictured above)

Leslie Knicl, Mahomet, Illinois

On the outside, they look like traditional brownies. When people bite in, though, they are surprised! It's almost like eating a rich filled chocolate candy.

1/2 cup butter (no substitutes)
1-1/4 cups semisweet chocolate chips
2 eggs
3/4 cup packed brown sugar
1 teaspoon instant coffee crystals
2 tablespoons water
1/2 teaspoon baking powder
3/4 cup all-purpose flour
FILLING:
1 cup (6 ounces) semisweet chocolate chips
1 package (8 ounces) cream cheese, softened
1/4 cup confectioners' sugar
1/3 cup seedless red raspberry jam

Soup Garnishes

ADDING a garnish to soup before serving gives color and adds to the flavor and texture. Easy ideas include: finely chopped green onions or chives, minced fresh parsley, shredded cheddar cheese, grated or shredded Parmesan cheese, a dollop of sour cream and plain or seasoned croutons.

Holiday Pecan Logs

(Pictured above)

Maxine Ruhl, Fort Scott, Kansas

For over 50 years, I've turned to this beloved recipe to make candy to give away at Christmas.

  2 teaspoons plus 1/2 cup butter (no substitutes), softened, *divided*
3-3/4 cups confectioners' sugar
  1/2 cup instant nonfat dry milk powder
  1/2 cup sugar
  1/2 cup light corn syrup
  1 teaspoon vanilla extract
  1 package (14 ounces) caramels
  1 tablespoon milk *or* half-and-half cream
  2 cups chopped pecans

Butter an 8-in. square pan with 2 teaspoons butter; set aside. Combine confectioners' sugar and milk powder; set aside. In a heavy saucepan, combine 1/2 cup butter, sugar and corn syrup; cook and stir until sugar is dissolved and mixture comes to a boil. Stir in confectioners' sugar mixture, about a third at a time, until blended. Remove from the heat; stir in vanilla. Continue stirring until the mixture mounds slightly when dropped from a spoon. Spread into prepared pan. Cool.

Cut candy into four strips; cut each strip in half. Shape each into a log; wrap in waxed paper and twist ends. Freeze or refrigerate until firm.

In a microwave or heavy saucepan, melt caramels with milk, stirring often. Roll logs in caramel mixture, then in pecans. Wrap in waxed paper. Store at room temperature in airtight containers. Cut into slices with a serrated knife. **Yield:** about 3-1/4 pounds.

Garlic Cheese Bread

Mike Marratzo, Florence, Alabama

I spent 11 years fixing daily meals for hundreds of workers on offshore oil rigs. So I know that meals for crowds

need to be simple to prepare, hot and filling. One of my favorites is this bread. I hope you enjoy serving it as much as I have over the years.

  6 cups grated Parmesan cheese
  1 cup dried oregano
  1 cup dried parsley flakes
  3 cups butter *or* margarine, softened
 12 garlic cloves, minced
  3 cups vegetable oil
 18 loaves French bread, cut into 1/2-inch slices
 18 pounds mozzarella cheese, shredded

Combine Parmesan, oregano and parsley; mix well and set aside. In a large mixing bowl, beat butter and garlic. Gradually beat in oil until smooth. Spread over one side of bread. Place with buttered side up in greased large shallow baking pans. Top each slice with 1/4 cup mozzarella. Sprinkle with Parmesan mixture. Bake at 400° for 10-12 minutes or until the cheese is melted and top is lightly browned. Serve warm. **Yield:** about 150 servings (2 slices each).

Classic Red Beans and Rice

Shirley Johnson, Kenner, Louisiana

This regional favorite has broad appeal because it is hearty and tasty but not too hot.

  6 pounds dry red kidney beans, sorted and rinsed
 18 garlic cloves, minced
  6 bay leaves
1-1/2 teaspoons browning sauce, optional
  2 pounds sliced bacon, diced
  3 pounds fully cooked smoked sausage, halved and cut into 1/4-inch slices
1-1/2 pounds cubed fully cooked ham
  1 cup vegetable oil
  2 cups all-purpose flour
  6 medium onions, chopped
  6 green onions, chopped
  6 celery ribs, chopped
  3 green peppers, chopped
  1/2 cup minced fresh parsley
  1/3 cup salt
  2 tablespoons pepper
 22 cups hot cooked rice
Hot pepper sauce, optional

Place beans in large kettles; add water to cover by 2 in. Bring to a boil; boil for 2 minutes. Remove from heat. Cover and let stand for 1 hour. Drain and discard liquid. To beans, add 9 qts. water, garlic, bay leaves and browning sauce if desired. Bring to a boil. Reduce heat; cover and simmer 1-1/2 to 2 hours or until beans are tender.

Meanwhile, in large skillets, cook bacon until crisp. Remove with a slotted spoon to paper towels. In the drippings, cook the sausage and ham until lightly browned. Remove and set aside. Add oil to drippings in skillets. Stir in flour until smooth; cook and stir over medium heat until reddish brown, about 12-14 minutes. Add onions, celery and green peppers; cook and stir until tender. Stir into bean mixture. Add bacon, sausage, ham, parsley, salt and pepper. Bring to a boil. Reduce heat; cover and simmer for 30 minutes. Remove bay leaves. Serve over rice with hot sauce if desired. **Yield:** 65 servings (about 1 cup beans and 1/3 cup rice).

Beefy Vegetable Soup

Linda Yutzy, Middlefield, Ohio

With a mild-tasting tomato-based broth and lots of colorful vegetables, this savory soup is always a real crowd-pleaser.

        12 cups diced peeled potatoes
        12 cups frozen sliced carrots
        12 cups frozen peas
        12 cups frozen lima beans
        12 cups frozen cut green beans
         9 cups diced celery
         1 package (16 ounces) small shell macaroni
         4 quarts tomato sauce
         2 cans (32 ounces *each*) chicken broth
        10 pounds ground beef
         2 pounds ground turkey
         4 cups diced onions
         3 tablespoons salt
         2 tablespoons dried basil
    1-1/2 teaspoons pepper

In several large kettles, combine the first seven ingredients. Add water to cover. Add tomato sauce and broth. In other large kettles, cook the beef, turkey and onions until meat is no longer pink; drain. Add to vegetable mixture. Stir in salt, basil and pepper; bring to a boil. Reduce heat; cover and simmer for 1-1/2 hours or until celery is tender. **Yield:** 120 (1-cup) servings.

Spaghetti for 100

Marilyn Monroe, Lansing, Michigan

A club I belong to used this main dish for a fund-raising dinner. One man came 50 miles because he'd had the dinner the year before and liked it so much.

         6 pounds ground beef
         2 cups chopped onion
        16 garlic cloves, minced
        12 cans (29 ounces *each*) tomato sauce
         4 cans (18 ounces *each*) tomato paste
    1/4 cup salt
         3 tablespoons sugar
         2 tablespoons *each* Italian seasoning, dried basil
           and oregano
        13 pounds spaghetti, cooked and drained

In a large stock pot, cook beef, onion and garlic until meat is no longer pink; drain. Add tomato sauce and paste, salt, sugar and seasonings; bring to a boil. Reduce heat; cover and simmer for 2-3 hours, stirring occasionally. Serve over spaghetti. **Yield:** 100 servings (about 50 cups sauce).

Buttermilk Pan Rolls

Elaine Kellum, Anaktuvuk Pass, Alaska

I've made these rolls for family and at the Eskimo village school where I work. I've had many compliments, and people always ask me when I'm going to serve them again.

        18 to 23 cups all-purpose flour
         1 cup buttermilk blend powder
    1/2 cup sugar
         2 tablespoons salt
    4-1/2 teaspoons active dry yeast
         1 teaspoon baking soda
         7 cups warm water (120° to 130°)
         1 cup vegetable oil

Combine 15 cups flour, buttermilk powder, sugar, salt, yeast and baking soda. Add water and oil. Beat until smooth. Stir in enough remaining flour to form a soft dough.

Turn onto a floured surface; knead until smooth and elastic, about 10 minutes. Place in a greased bowl, turning once to grease top. Cover and let rise in a warm place until doubled, about 1-1/4 hours.

Punch dough down. Divide into 80 pieces. With lightly floured hands, shape each into a ball. Place in two greased 15-in. x 10-in. x 1-in. baking pans. Cover and let rise until doubled, about 30 minutes. Bake at 375° for 20-30 minutes or until lightly browned. Remove from pans to wire racks. **Yield:** 80 rolls.

Ham Balls

DeEtta Rasmussen, Olmsted, Illinois

These meatballs are baked in a thick tomato sauce laced with the sweet taste of brown sugar. I've made them for many church functions over the years...everyone just loves them! To save time, ask your butcher to grind together the ham, pork and beef. I also use an ice cream scoop to make the meatballs so there's no mess.

        10 pounds ground fully cooked ham
         8 pounds lean ground pork
         4 pounds lean ground beef
        12 eggs, beaten
        12 cups graham cracker crumbs
         6 cups milk
    SAUCE:
         8 cans (10-3/4 ounces *each*) condensed tomato
           soup, undiluted
         1 cup vinegar
         8 cups packed brown sugar
         3 tablespoons ground mustard

In a large bowl, combine ham, pork and beef; mix well. Add eggs; mix well. Blend in crumbs and milk. Form into 1-1/2-in. balls. Place in a single layer in 12 ungreased 13-in. x 9-in. x 2-in. baking pans or larger pans if available; set aside. In a bowl, combine sauce ingredients. Divide evenly among pans, covering the ham balls. Bake, uncovered, at 350° for 60 minutes or until hot and bubbly. **Yield:** 100 servings.

Gift Box Cake

This lovely cake designed by our Test Kitchen staff is almost too pretty to eat!

1-1/3 cups poppy seeds, *divided*
4 packages (18-1/4 ounces *each***) white cake mix**
1 package (3.4 ounces) instant lemon pudding mix
FROSTING:
1-1/2 cups butter (no substitutes), softened
15 cups confectioners' sugar
3/4 cup half-and-half cream
1-1/2 teaspoons vanilla extract
1/2 teaspoon salt
2 pastry bags *or* **heavy-duty resealable plastic bags**
Round pastry tips #3 and #5
Pink liquid *or* **paste food coloring**
4 covered cardboard bases (10 x 8, 8 x 8, 7 x 6 and 4 x 4 inches)
Dowel rods (1/4-inch diameter)
Ribbons and silk flowers, optional

In four bowls, soak 1/3 cup poppy seeds in the water required for each cake mix for 1 hour. Mix each cake according to package directions, using poppy seed water. Bake in three greased and floured 13-in. x 9-in. x 2-in. baking pans and two 8-in. square pans; cool. Prepare pudding according to package directions; chill.

For frosting, cream butter and sugar in a mixing bowl on low speed for 1 minute. Add cream, vanilla and salt; mix on medium until light and fluffy, about 3 minutes. (Frosting may need to be made in batches.) Add food coloring to 4-1/2 cups frosting.

Cut a small hole in the corner of two plastic or pastry bags; insert #3 pastry tip in one bag and #5 pastry tip in the other. Place 1/2 cup white frosting in bag with #3 tip and 1/2 cup pink frosting in the other. Cover remaining frosting with a damp cloth until ready to use.

Trim two 13-in. x 9-in. cakes into 12-in. x 8-in. rectangles as in Fig. 1a; level tops. Cut an 8-in. x 2-in. strip off each, leaving two pieces (A). Cut each strip in half, forming four 4-in. x 2-in. pieces. As in Fig. 1b, attach two 4-in. x 2-in. pieces together lengthwise with white frosting to form a 4-in. x 4-in. piece (B); repeat with two remaining pieces and set aside.

Trim remaining 13-in. x 9-in. cake into a 12-in. x 7-in. rectangle as in Fig. 2; level top. Cut cake in half to form two 7-in. x 6-in. pieces (C); set aside.

Level tops of 8-in. square cakes.

Each frosted layer of the cake consists of two cake pieces with a lemon pudding filling in between. Place one piece A on the largest covered board; spread with pudding to within 1/2 in. of edge. Place second piece A on top; set aside. Repeat filling procedure for remaining layers (pieces B, C and 8-in. squares) and place on covered boards.

For bottom layer, frost piece A with 3-1/2 cups white frosting. If desired, attach a ribbon across the corners of piece A (as shown in photo).

For second layer, frost 8-in. cake with 2-1/2 cups pink frosting. With prepared bag of white frosting, pipe a continuous string, curving up, down and around so strings never touch or cross on cake.

For third layer, frost piece C with 2 cups white frosting. With prepared bag of pink frosting, pipe dots 1/2 in. apart over entire cake.

Frost piece B with remaining pink frosting. Add bow on top.

For bottom three layers, cut a dowel into five pieces the height of each layer. Insert dowels 1 to 2 in. apart in center of each cake to support the next layer. Carefully stack layers on a serving platter, working from the largest cake to the smallest. Decorate with ribbon and silk flowers as desired. Remove dowels before cutting layers. **Yield:** 50 servings.

Editor's Note: Unfrosted cakes can be frozen for up to 6 months wrapped in foil. Frosting can be prepared 2 weeks ahead; store in the refrigerator. Rewhip before spreading. Cake can be assembled 8 hours before serving.

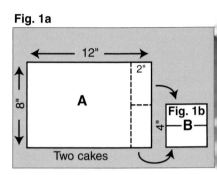
Fig. 1a

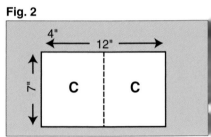
Fig. 2

Garden Layered Salad

It's easy to feed a crowd with this impressive-looking salad from our Test Kitchen. It's made ahead, leaving you time for last-minute party details.

12 cups broccoli florets
9 cups cauliflowerets
6 cups sliced fresh mushrooms
3 cups halved sugar snap peas
3 cups sliced radishes
3 cups sliced carrots
3 cups fresh *or* **frozen peas**
3/4 cup sliced green onions
2-1/4 cups olive *or* **vegetable oil**
1 cup red wine vinegar *or* **cider vinegar**
6 tablespoons sugar
1/3 cup minced fresh chives
1 tablespoon pepper
1 tablespoon Dijon mustard
1-1/2 teaspoons salt
3 garlic cloves, minced
6 quarts assorted torn greens

In a large bowl, toss the first eight ingredients. Whisk the oil, vinegar, sugar, chives, pepper, mustard, salt and garlic; pour over vegetables and toss. Place 1 qt. of greens in three 4-qt. bowls; top each with 6 cups vegetable mixture. Repeat layers. Cover and refrigerate for at least 6 hours. **Yield:** 50 servings.

CELEBRATING special occasions will be a breeze when you rely on Rosy Rhubarb Mold, Chicken Wild Rice Dish, Garden Layered Salad and Gift Box Cake (clockwise from front right).

Chicken Wild Rice Dish

Our Test Kitchen staff came up with this easy-but-elegant main dish that'll serve 50. Simply double the recipe, and you can feed 100!

        2 pounds sliced fresh mushrooms
        4 cups chopped celery
        4 cups chopped sweet red pepper
    2-2/3 cups chopped green onions
        8 garlic cloves, minced
    1-1/3 cups butter *or* margarine
        4 cans (14-1/2 ounces *each*) chicken broth
       24 cups cubed cooked chicken
       16 cups cooked wild rice
       16 cups cooked long grain rice
        8 cups (2 pounds) shredded cheddar cheese
        3 tablespoons salt
        3 tablespoons dried basil
        2 teaspoons pepper

In a kettle, saute the first five ingredients in butter until tender. Add remaining ingredients; mix well. Spoon into four greased 13-in. x 9-in. x 2-in. baking dishes. Cover and bake at 350° for 75 minutes. Uncover; bake 15 minutes longer or until heated through. **Yield:** 50 servings.

Editor's Note: This dish may be assembled and refrigerated overnight. Remove from the refrigerator 1 hour before baking.

Rosy Rhubarb Mold

This pretty gelatin mold from our Test Kitchen is an eye-catching way to round out a buffet table.

       24 cups chopped rhubarb
        6 cups water
        3 cups sugar
        6 packages (6 ounces *each*) strawberry gelatin
        3 cups orange juice
        2 tablespoons grated orange peel
        6 cups sliced fresh strawberries
    Leaf lettuce
    Additional strawberries
        3 cups mayonnaise
        3 cups whipped topping
        6 to 7 tablespoons milk

In a kettle over medium-low heat, cook and stir rhubarb, water and sugar until rhubarb is soft and tender. Remove from the heat; stir in gelatin until dissolved. Stir in orange juice and peel. Chill until partially set, about 2-3 hours. Stir in strawberries. Pour into six 5-cup ring molds coated with nonstick cooking spray. Refrigerate overnight. Unmold onto lettuce-lined platters; garnish with berries.

For dressing, combine mayonnaise and whipped topping; add enough milk to thin to desired consistency. Serve in a bowl in center of mold. **Yield:** 50 servings.

Punch Bowl Trifle

Margaret Wagner Allen, Abingdon, Virginia

This impresive-looking trifle is an easy way to serve a big group a little different dessert.

- 2 cans (20 ounces *each*) crushed pineapple
- 1 package (18-1/4 ounces) yellow cake mix
- 1 package (5.1 ounces) instant vanilla pudding mix
- 2 cans (21 ounces *each*) cherry pie filling
- 4 medium ripe bananas, sliced
- 2 cans (15-1/4 ounces *each*) fruit cocktail, drained
- 2 cans (11 ounces *each*) mandarin oranges, drained
- 1 carton (16 ounces) frozen whipped topping, thawed
- 1 package (7 ounces) flaked coconut, toasted

Drain pineapple, reserving juice; set the pineapple aside. Prepare cake batter according to package directions, substituting pineapple juice for the water (add water if necessary for the required measurement). Bake as directed in a greased 13-in. x 9-in. x 2-in. pan. Cool.

Meanwhile, prepare pudding according to package directions. Cut the cake into 1-in. cubes; place half in a 6-qt. punch bowl. Top with half of the pudding, pie filling, pineapple, bananas, fruit cocktail, oranges, whipped topping and coconut. Repeat layers. Cover and chill for 6 hours or overnight. **Yield:** 55 (1/2-cup) servings.

Turkey Salad for 60

Terry Smith, Campbell Hall, New York

The mild seasonings in this turkey salad certainly have mass appeal.

- 1 turkey (20 to 22 pounds)
- 4 packages (7 ounces *each*) ring macaroni, cooked and drained
- 3 bunches celery, thinly sliced
- 3 cans (8 ounces *each*) sliced water chestnuts, drained
- 2 packages (16 ounces *each*) frozen tiny sweet peas, thawed
- 1 large onion, diced
- 2 quarts mayonnaise
- 2 tablespoons seasoned salt
- 4 cups slivered almonds, toasted

Roast the turkey. Cool; debone and cut into chunks. Combine turkey, macaroni, celery, water chestnuts, peas and onion. Combine the mayonnaise and seasoned salt; stir into the salad. Chill for several hours. Add almonds just before serving. **Yield:** 60 servings.

Boston Cream Pie

Clara Honeyager, Mukwonago, Wisconsin

This delectable dessert can be made without much fuss. It's pretty tasty and very popular.

- 4 packages (18-1/4 ounces *each*) yellow cake mix
- 11 cups cold milk
- 4 packages (5.1 ounces *each*) instant vanilla pudding mix
- 4 jars (16 ounces *each*) hot fudge topping, warmed

Prepare cake mixes according to package directions. Bake in four greased 13-in. x 9-in. x 2-in. baking pans; cool. In a mixing bowl, beat milk and pudding mixes on low for 2-3 minutes. Cover; chill for 30 minutes. Cut each cake into 24 pieces; split each piece horizontally. Place 1 heaping tablespoon of pudding between layers. Top with 1 tablespoon fudge topping. **Yield:** 96 servings.

Cheesy Corn Squares

Peggy Paul, Florence, South Carolina

My family loves corn, and I love to come up with new ways to fix it. I created this recipe a couple of years ago.

- 1-1/4 cups all-purpose flour
- 2 tablespoons minced fresh parsley
- 1 teaspoon baking soda
- 1 teaspoon seasoned salt
- 1/2 teaspoon dried basil
- 1/2 teaspoon dried oregano
- 1/2 teaspoon pepper
- 4 eggs, beaten
- 1 can (15-1/4 ounces) whole kernel corn, drained
- 1 cup ricotta cheese
- 1/3 cup finely chopped onion
- 1/4 cup grated Parmesan cheese
- 1/4 cup vegetable oil
- 2 cups (8 ounces) shredded mozzarella cheese, *divided*
- 1 teaspoon paprika

In a large bowl, combine the first seven ingredients. Stir in eggs, corn, ricotta, onion, Parmesan, oil and 1-1/2 cups of mozzarella; mix well. Pour into a greased 13-in. x 9-in. x 2-in. baking pan. Sprinkle with paprika and remaining mozzarella. Bake, uncovered, at 350° for 30-35 minutes or until golden brown. **Yield:** 5 dozen.

Cranberry Punch

Elaine Schlender, Clintonville, Wisconsin

Tingle taste buds with this rosy punch that perfectly suits the holiday season.

- 3 pints honey
- 3 quarts hot tea
- 4 bottles (48 ounces *each*) cranberry juice
- 1 gallon orange juice
- 3 pints lemon juice
- 4 bottles (2 liters *each*) grapefruit-lime soda, chilled

Dissolve honey in tea. Cool. Add cranberry, orange and lemon juices; chill. Just before serving, add soda. **Yield:** 90-95 servings (about 1/2 cup each).

INDEX

This handy index lists every recipe by food category and/or major ingredient,
so you can easily locate recipes to suit your needs.

 Recipe includes Nutritional Analysis and Diabetic Exchanges

✓ Recipe includes Nutritional Analysis and Diabetic Exchanges

✓ Recipe includes Nutritional Analysis and Diabetic Exchanges

✓ Recipe includes Nutritional Analysis and Diabetic Exchanges